P9-DTB-260

annoying

annoying

THE SCIENCE OF WHAT BUGS US

JOE PALCA AND FLORA LICHTMAN

WILEY

John Wiley & Sons, Inc.

Copyright © 2011 by Joe Palca and Flora Lichtman. All rights reserved

Published by John Wiley & Sons, Inc., Hoboken, New Jersey
Published simultaneously in Canada

No part of this publication may be reproduced, stored in a retrieval system, or transmitted in any form or by any means, electronic, mechanical, photocopying, recording, scanning, or otherwise, except as permitted under Section 107 or 108 of the 1976 United States Copyright Act, without either the prior written permission of the Publisher, or authorization through payment of the appropriate per-copy fee to the Copyright Clearance Center, 222 Rosewood Drive, Danvers, MA 01923, (978) 750-8400, fax (978) 646-8600, or on the web at www.copyright.com. Requests to the Publisher for permission should be addressed to the Permissions Department, John Wiley & Sons, Inc., 111 River Street, Hoboken, NJ 07030, (201) 748-6011, fax (201) 748-6008, or online at http://www.wiley.com/go/permissions.

Limit of Liability/Disclaimer of Warranty: While the publisher and the author have used their best efforts in preparing this book, they make no representations or warranties with respect to the accuracy or completeness of the contents of this book and specifically disclaim any implied warranties of merchantability or fitness for a particular purpose. No warranty may be created or extended by sales representatives or written sales materials. The advice and strategies contained herein may not be suitable for your situation. You should consult with a professional where appropriate. Neither the publisher nor the author shall be liable for any loss of profit or any other commercial damages, including but not limited to special, incidental, consequential, or other damages.

For general information about our other products and services, please contact our Customer Care Department within the United States at (800) 762-2974, outside the United States at (317) 572-3993 or fax (317) 572-4002.

Wiley also publishes its books in a variety of electronic formats. Some content that appears in print may not be available in electronic books. For more information about Wiley products, visit our web site at www.wiley.com.

Library of Congress Cataloging-in-Publication Data:

Palca, Joe.
  Annoying : the science of what bugs us / Joe Palca and Flora Lichtman.
      p. cm.
  Includes bibliographical references and index.
  ISBN 978-0-470-63869-9 (hardback); ISBN 978-1-118-02809-4 (ebk.);
ISBN 978-1-118-02810-0 (ebk.); ISBN 978-1-118-02811-7 (ebk.)
1. Aversive stimuli—Physiological effect. 2. Aversion—Psyiological aspects.
3. Neuropsychology. 4. Discontent. 5. Human physiology. I. Lichtman, Flora. Title.
  QP401.P35 2011
  612.8—dc22   2010054046

Printed in the United States of America

10 9 8 7 6 5 4 3 2 1

To our families

Contents

A Note from the Authors

The trouble with investigating the science of annoyance is that unlike simple topics such as string theory or molecular genetics, the science of what's annoying is highly complex, drawing on multiple disciplines from physics, chemistry, and biology in the natural sciences to psychology, sociology, anthropology, and linguistics in the social sciences to history, literature, philosophy, and art in the humanities.

Indeed, the expert in annoyingness, if such a person existed, would be a true polymath. Of course, we all have some expertise in the sensation—both in generating it in others and feeling it within ourselves. In fact, when you tell somebody you're writing a book about the science of what's annoying—after you get the guffaws out of the way—you often hear a long diatribe about the annoying thing that happened just the other day. It's paradoxical—we don't like being annoyed but seem to enjoy thinking about what annoys us. Although everyone can tell you what's annoying, few, if any, can explain why. That's why we turned to science.

It may seem like a trivial pursuit, but think about it for a moment. Feeling annoyed seems to be a universal trait. Can you think of anyone who is immune to it? Although as a species modern humans appear to have become exquisitely sensitive to annoyances, other species look to be at risk as well. While animal behaviorists and microbiologists may disagree with the terminology, it's difficult to argue with the statement that at least something remarkably similar to annoyance occurs across a broad swath of the animal kingdom. Older dogs become annoyed with pesky puppies; fruit flies are smart enough to avoid irritants; even bacteria will switch on their flagellums and move away when faced with the microbiological equivalent of fingernails on a blackboard. In the great tradition of reductionism, understanding these annoyances will surely tell us something about our own.

Although little direct research has been conducted on the topic, there's no shortage of relevant data: science has a lot to say about annoyance. In our quest to understand this feeling, we came across some patterns that help explain what makes something annoying. Don't expect a proof for a Grand Unified Theory of Annoyance; this is a scientific field in its infancy. We offer our findings as a place to start.

Introduction: Cell Phones

I t can happen to anyone, at any time, in any place—in public bathrooms, on trains, in schools, even in your own backyard. You're never safe. For Mark Liberman, a linguist at the University of Pennsylvania, it happened at the gym. "There was a young woman on the treadmill next to mine who was talking on her cell phone, and I was doing my best to tune it out, but she kept saying the same sentence over and over and over again. It was something like, 'He's arriving tomorrow.' I think she must have said it like ten or twelve times."

This is a classic case of cell phone annoyance. Liberman couldn't ignore the broken record on the treadmill next to him, and that was annoying. Why? Maybe it was annoying because talking on a cell phone when you're in a public space is rude.

Why is it rude? Lauren Emberson, a psychology graduate student who studied this, has an answer. "I think the reason why is that we can't tune it out. We find it more rude than someone having a conversation around us because our attention is drawn in and that makes us irritated that we can't be doing the other things or thinking about the other things that we want to. That's why it seems intrusive."[1]

It's an interesting idea: what we find rude is what we cannot ignore. In terms of cell phone conversations, Liberman points out that some will be harder to ignore than others—louder conversations will be more annoying, and the content of certain conversations may be more attention grabbing.

If you think it's juicy content that keeps people tuned in to others' cell calls, however, think again. The most mundane cell phone conversation, as Liberman found out at the gym, can be the hardest to ignore. "It was maddening because I couldn't figure what could be going on that was causing her to repeat the same thing over and over again," Liberman says. "It wasn't in itself very interesting; what was attention-getting was the unexpected fact of repetition. What was the conversational setting that would lead to this?"

This perfectly embodies Emberson's theory of what makes a cell phone conversation—which she and her coauthors dub a "halfalogue"—annoying. The repetition of the girl on the treadmill was annoying because it was distracting. It was distracting because, try as we might—and we do try—we can't even imagine how that conversation would make any sense.

•   •   •

The neighborhoods nearest to the campus of the University of British Columbia at Vancouver are expensive—too expensive for students, says Emberson, who was a student there and didn't live near campus. She lived a forty-five-minute bus ride away, which translated to a lot of commuting, which translated to a lot of reading.

When Emberson was in college, cell phones were just starting to get popular. She didn't have one, and they annoyed her, especially on the bus. She wanted to read her essays on the philosophy of mind, but she found herself distracted by her bus-mates' conversations. "Being an academic, I couldn't stop at just being irritated," she recalls. "I started thinking, 'Why was I irritated?' I couldn't tune it out, and I used to think it was because I was nosy. But I actually didn't want to listen. I felt myself forced to, almost. For most people, that's not enough to go and do a study about it." It was for Emberson, though, who is now at Cornell University. She devised a study to test her hypothesis on why cell phone conversations are so irritating.[2]

Everyone is annoyed by something. Many of us are annoyed by lots of things. Most of these annoyances have more to do with our personal sensitivities—our neuroses, our upbringings, our points of view—than any objective "annoying" quality. Other annoyances are so powerful, however, that they transcend race, gender, age, and culture. At the top of the list is that most convenient of modern conveniences, the cell phone—at least, when someone *else* is talking on it.

Researchers at the University of York have shown that cell phone chatter is particularly annoying compared to conversations in which listeners can hear both sides.[3] You don't need to have a special sensitivity, it's not a matter of taste, it doesn't have to remind you of something, and it's not an intrinsic feature of the human voice. Cell phone conversations are different. Could there be something about this annoyance that taps into the essence of our humanness?

Emberson has a theory. "It actually happened to fit into my emerging worldview about how we respond to information around us," she says. Her view is that when we hear half a conversation, such as when someone is talking on a cell phone, "our brains are always predicting what's going to happen next, based on our current state of knowledge—this is how we learn about the world, but it also reflects how we are in the world. When something is unexpected, it draws our attention in, our brains tune into it because we're this information-seeking, prediction-loving cognitive system—this is the idea."

Although cell phones are fairly new, halfalogues aren't a new annoyance. More than a century ago, Mark Twain railed against them. Twain was a man, let it be said, who found no shortage of annoyances in life, and American literature is all the richer for it. In 1880—just four years after Alexander Graham Bell first exhibited his telephone at the Centennial Exposition in Philadelphia—Twain wrote an essay called "A Telephonic Conversation," in which he stated,

> Consider that a conversation by telephone—when you are simply sitting by and not taking any part in that conversation—is one of the solemnest curiosities of this modern life. Yesterday I was writing a deep article on a sublime philosophical subject while such a conversation was going on in the room. . . . You hear questions asked; you don't hear

the answer. You hear invitations given; you hear no thanks in return. You have listening pauses of dead silence, followed by apparently irrelevant and unjustifiable exclamations of glad surprise or sorrow or dismay. You can't make head or tail of the talk, because you never hear anything that the person at the other end of the wire says.[4]

As Twain put it, you "can't make head or tail of the talk," and Emberson thinks this is the root of why cell phone conversations so effectively capture our attention—and subsequently annoy us. When you hear only half of a conversation, it's hard to predict when the person will start talking again and what that person is going to say when he does open his mouth.

Part of the recipe for what makes something annoying seems to be its level of unpredictability. Completely random stimuli, we can tune out. We also have an easier time ignoring something that is steady, stable, and routine. But things that have some pattern, like the rhythm of a conversation, but are not predictable—grab our attention, whether we want them to or not.

Speech, especially, reels us in. You might think that when you're having a conversation with someone your brain is focused on listening, on taking in what that person is saying and processing the information he's imparting. You probably think you're absorbing his words like a sponge and possibly preparing your response. In fact, your brain is focused on guessing what the person is going to say next. You may be able to finish your spouse's sentences, but your mind wants to finish *everyone's* sentences.

Humans are always trying to predict speech, says Liberman. It relates to an idea called "theory of mind," which suggests that people can't help themselves from trying to read into what other people are thinking. "It's also pretty much automatic," he wrote on his blog Language Log.[5] "If you're not autistic, you can't stop yourself from reading your companions' minds any more than you can stop yourself from noticing the color of their clothes." This applies to conversations, too, he says: if you're listening to half of a conversation, "then filling in all this theory of mind stuff does seem to be unavoidable."

Humans are pretty good at filling in the blanks. One experimental paradigm that tests our brains' ability to predict language has to do with *verbal shadowing*. "The task is to listen to someone speaking and repeat what they say as soon as possible after they say it," says Liberman. "There used to be people who would go on variety shows because they could do it almost as fast as the person was talking. They hardly seemed to be behind them at all. But everyone can do this to some extent with a lag of a few tenths of a second."

As the speech becomes more unpredictable—or what Liberman calls "word salad—just random words spoken in sequence—the shadowing lag is very long compared to semantically incoherent but syntactically well-formed, nonsense material." The shadowing rate gets better and better as the structure and the content of the speech become more coherent.

Theories about how our brains prefer predictability show up in music research, too. "What we know from a biological perspective is that the best surprise is no surprise," says musicologist David Huron. "Large parts of your brain are oriented toward predicting what's going to happen next. There are excellent biological adaptive reasons why brains should be so oriented toward what's going to happen. An accurate prediction is rewarded by the brain. It's one of the reasons why in music we have very predictive rhythms. The thing to say about music is that it's incredibly repetitive."

Emberson tested the idea that halfalogues distract us more than dialogues or monologues do by asking people to listen to half of a cell phone conversation while performing a task that required paying attention. To make the cell phone conversations as realistic as possible, Emberson and her colleagues gathered Cornell undergrad roommates, brought them to the lab, and recorded them chatting to one another on their phones. Then the researchers asked them to sum up the conversations in monologues. This provided the researchers with halfalogues, dialogues, and monologues to play to listeners.

Listeners were asked to perform two tasks: The first was to keep a mouse cursor on a dot that was moving around a computer screen—which requires constant monitoring. The other was to hold four letters in memory and hit a button any time one of the letters popped up on the screen and refrain from hitting that button when another letter popped up. These tasks required monitoring and decision making. "Both demand a great deal of attention, but in very different ways," says Emberson. "We wanted to know if there was an attentional effect for the different types of speech."

The distraction of the conversations caused an effect, the researchers reported in the journal *Psychological Science*.[6] During the mouse tracker task, people started to make more errors in the moments after the halfalogue recommenced. "When the person starts talking, your attention is really drawn in," says Emberson. "It's really automatic." The errors occurred in the 400 milliseconds after the audible speech restarted. It almost seemed reflexive.

Would any blast of random noise derail us? To make sure the effect was specifically caused by understandable speech, Emberson filtered the halfalogue so that it was garbled. She says it sounded like someone talking underwater. You could tell it was speech, but you couldn't make out the content. In that case, the distracting effects went away. When the halfalogue speech was incomprehensible, people didn't screw up the task.

When people performed the letter-matching task, Emberson found that people did worse when they were hearing a halfalogue compared with a dialogue or a monologue, which may suggest that we're more distracted by halfalogues generally. Emberson interprets the findings to mean that "there's a cost when you can't predict the succession of speech."

Liberman generally agrees with the theory that halfalogues are more distracting than dialogues or monologues: "It's extremely well-established, something that Emberson and company have assumed; when you're getting lower-quality information coming in, you're having to work harder to understand and reconstruct it." Liberman is more cautious about whether the increased cognitive load from unpredictable content is solely responsible for the decrease in performance on the attention tasks.

That brings us to our second ingredient in the recipe for what's annoying. Whatever it is—a buzzing mosquito, a pestering child, a dripping faucet, or half of a cell phone conversation—it has to be unpleasant. Not horrible, not deadly, just mildly discomfiting. Whether halfalogues are distracting because they're rude or rude because they're distracting, it's rare to listen to someone else's cell phone conversation and enjoy it. Some things are inherently unpleasant—the sound of fingernails on a chalkboard probably falls in this category—and others are more unique to the individual. Some people find being stuck in traffic unpleasant; others don't seem to mind a bit.

Overheard cell phone conversations point to a third and final ingredient in the perfect recipe for annoyance: the certainty that it *will* end, but the uncertainty of *when.* To be annoyed requires some impatience on your part. The conversation could be finished in a few more seconds, or maybe it will stretch on for another hour—it's the knowledge that the unpleasantness will come to an end soon that gives a particular situation an edge, a sense of urgency. That is, your annoyance is related to your sense of optimism. Your hope that it will be over amplifies every additional second that you have to put up with it.

Annoyance is probably the most widely experienced and least studied of all human emotions. How do we know that? We don't really. There is no Department of Annoying Studies or annoyingologists. There are no data, no measurements of how many people are annoyed or how annoyed people are, no investigations into what makes people annoyed, and no systematic looks at how people cope with annoyance. In fact, if you talk to psychologists, practitioners of a scientific discipline that one would think would have grappled with annoyance, you get the feeling that there might not be such a thing as annoyance at all.

So we set out to try to understand this feeling by min-
ing the science in every field. There's no dearth of relevant
research. A vast literature exists on anger, aversion, acoustics,
social anthropology, and chemical irritants, but few scientists
have thought about these things in terms of how they help
explain annoyance. That's what this book sets out to do. Buzzing flies, car alarms, skunk odors, bad habits, terrible music,
idiotic employers, recalcitrant spouses, and more. Tell people
you're writing a book on the annoyingness of modern life, and
you'll soon realize what a tetchy species we humans are.

Cell phones aside, the trouble with cataloging annoyances is that there seem to be few universals in what we find
unpleasant. You may like the smell of aftershave, whereas it
annoys your spouse. Pleasures can become pet peeves. You
may find your spouse's way of using a knife cute when you
first get together and god-awfully annoying after twenty years
of marriage. The experience of annoyance is so subjective, so
context dependent, that it's hard to nail down. This may be
why researchers don't tend to think of annoyance as a separate
emotion. "From my perspective, annoyance is mild anger,"
says James Gross, a psychologist at Stanford University. "And
there's a huge literature on anger." Paul Rozin, a psychologist at the University of Pennsylvania, warns, "You have to
be careful to distinguish annoyance from aversion." "It's hard
to distinguish annoyance from frustration," says University of
Florida psychologist Clive Wynne.

Emotions are sometimes plotted on a chart with positive/
negative on one axis and arousal/calm on the other axis.
"Annoyance would be arousal-negative. But it's a subtle one,
isn't it?" asks Dr. Randolph Nesse, a psychiatrist and the
director of the Evolution and Human Adaptation Program at

the University of Michigan. "It's not quite rage. It's not quite anger. It doesn't fit real nicely on those valences." Annoyance seems to be its own thing. It's possible that defining annoyance is as difficult as Justice Potter Stewart found defining pornography to be: "I know it when I see it." Knowing it when you see it, however, isn't always good enough. In some lines of work, you need to be an expert in being annoying just to get through the day.

I

A Noise Annoys

Summer 2010 was a hot one for New York City. Spring came early, and once the warm weather set in, it didn't lift for most of the summer. A heat wave in July brought temperatures to the triple digits for several days, in and around town. People were desperate for relief. Hydrants were hacked; hoses, uncoiled. Side streets became mini water parks. Pool admissions were up.

July 6 was the real scorcher. It reached 103 degrees that day—breaking an eight-year record. According to the *New York Daily News*, since 1869, when officials began to keep temperature records in New York City, only three days have been hotter.

That was a busy day for the New York Fire Department's Emergency Medical Service. It received 4,225 calls, about 30 percent more than usual, the *New York Times* reported. It was the fifth busiest day for the service in eight years.

When you call 911 in New York City, you first talk to a call-receiving operator called a CRO. (There are a lot of annoying acronyms in emergency medicine.) The CRO is trained to ask a series of questions to determine whether the emergency requires medical attention. If it does, an emergency medical services (EMS) dispatcher—who is trained as an emergency medical technician (EMT)—gets conferenced into the call. The EMS dispatcher determines what level of response is required: the most serious calls—"segment 1s"—are choking, cardiac or respiratory arrest, and drowning. Segment 1s always get two paramedics, two EMTs, and a team of certified first responders (CFRs), plus the cops often show up.

The New York EMS is run by the Fire Department (FDNY). The FDNY is responsible for first-response care for more than seven million people over three hundred square miles of the New York metropolitan area. It responds to more than a million medical emergencies every year. At any given time, 250 ambulances are on the street. That number can seem even higher if your apartment has street-facing windows.

Will Tung is an FDNY paramedic in Brooklyn. He's in his late twenties and is also the president of the Park Slope Volunteer Ambulance Corps (PSVAC), which is located in the basement of a narrow brick building on a tree-lined street on the fringe of downtown Brooklyn and the neighborhood of Park Slope. The PSVAC responded to more than five hundred emergencies last year—from direct phone calls or through calls from the FDNY in times of high call volume. With thirty-six active members, the corps is made up entirely of volunteers. It was started back in the early 1990s, when people were concerned about the lagging response times for EMS in the neighborhood. Someone is standing by on most nights. During the day, you get a voice message instructing you to call 911 if you're looking for help.

In 2009, the average response time for FDNY EMS calls was eight minutes, twenty-seven seconds. In addition to choking and cardiac and respiratory arrests, the most serious calls included snakebites, asthma attacks, gunshots, stabbings, major burns, electrocution, and other traumas. The average response time for these calls was six minutes, forty-one seconds.

If you've ever driven in New York City, you know that getting anywhere in six minutes is a remarkable feat. It can take that long to get out of your parking spot, let alone across town. EMS vehicles, of course, are equipped with tools to help them part the automotive seas—namely, lights and sirens.

The original siren was part lady, part monster, and had a knack for luring men by means of irresistible song. The word has taken on new meaning since then—nowadays, most people would not say they're irresistibly drawn to sirens.

Sirens are designed to be annoying. If they didn't get your attention or you could tune them out, they would not be effective. If you find sirens irritating, just imagine what it's like for people inside the siren-equipped vehicle. "Sirens are really annoying," says Tung. "When you're a pedestrian, it passes." For everybody in the ambulance, it doesn't go away. Tung generally keeps the windows rolled up to cut down on noise. When the windows are open and the siren is blasting, it's hard to hear anything else.

•   •   •

Sirens are related to another particularly modern kind of annoyance: the intrusive electronic beeps and blips from appliances, computers, phones, and other devices on which we depend. As annoying (and useful) as many of those can be, no one is ever glad to hear an electronic beep that they can't quite place.

Picture the scene: it's Christmastime in a Detroit suburb. Christmas is a wonderful time of the year and also a supremely annoying time of year. Airports are choked. So are roads. Stores are full of desperate shoppers continually frustrated by the endless search for the perfect gift.

Yet if there are certain annoyances intrinsic to holidays, it takes a special kind of person to insert an additional annoyance on purpose. You can find such a person at the annual Christmas gathering at the home of Bob and Sue Johnson. The Johnson family really exists; we simply changed some names.

The house is a sprawling affair. There is a large, sunken dining room with a two-story ceiling. Even an eight-foot-tall Christmas tree sitting on a table is swallowed by the room's vastness.

On the south wall, picture windows reveal a large yard, and because this is Michigan in the winter, the yard is usually obligingly covered with snow. The Johnsons' three children and seven grandchildren do a pretty good job of occupying every corner of the house.

Uncle Ted takes Christmas very seriously, especially the assembling of Christmas stockings. Each year, he brings a bag of stocking stuffers. The bag contains candy, the latest squoosh ball, and the occasional key chain with a miniature Swiss Army knife or nameplate attached.

Ted is a bit of a gadget geek and usually finds some low-cost but high-tech toy to throw into the mix. For Christmas 2009, Ted introduced his extended family to what must be considered the perfect toy for this book: the Annoy-a-tron.

The Annoy-a-tron is made of a small piece of printed circuit board about the size of a quarter. In addition to the on-off switch, there is a small speaker and a magnet.

The Annoy-a-tron generates a short (but eponymously annoying) beep at random intervals every few minutes. Given its size and the short duration of the beep, figuring out where the noise is coming from is extremely difficult. Because the noise is soft, you're not quite sure you heard it. Because the noise is random, you can't predict when it will occur. So even if you become obsessed with finding the source, it will take an annoyingly long time to pinpoint it.

The Annoy-a-tron has the requisite ingredients to be annoying: it's unpleasant, it's unpredictable, and it leads you to falsely believe that it will end any second. It is especially ingenious because it's only barely unpleasant. It's not exactly cruel, although it's so unpredictable and just beyond reach that it's perfectly torturous.

For the Annoy-a-tron, you can choose between two different frequencies for the beep tone. According to the sales literature, the "2 kHz sound is generically annoying enough, but if you really, really want to aggravate somebody, select the 12 kHz sound. Trust us." The higher frequency and the slight "electronic noise" built into that beep tone is really grating.

Now, Uncle Ted is a sweet guy. He's patient and loving with his parents, generous with his nieces and nephews, and helpful in the kitchen. Yet that didn't stop him on Christmas day from attaching an Annoy-a-tron to the underside of the metal frame of the coffee table in the living room and switching it on.

Even though most of the gathering knew about the Annoy-a-tron, at least those who had carefully examined the contents of their Christmas stockings, people still seemed miffed by the occasional muffled beeping. At first, it was simply confusing.

"Did you hear something?"

"I think so."

"I didn't."

"There it is again."

"I heard it that time."

"Where's it coming from?"

After half an hour, Ted took pity on those who hadn't figured out what was happening. After all, he's a sweet guy.

The reason the Annoy-a-tron is hard to locate probably has more to do with the brevity of the tone than the frequency. We humans with two working ears are pretty good at determining where a sound is coming from. Except for really low tones or sounds that are directly in front of us, the sound will be slightly louder in the ear that is closer to sound than in the one farther away. That's because some of the sound is absorbed by our (thick) heads. Lucas C. Parra, a professor of biomedical engineering at the City College of the City University of New York, says that by swiveling our heads, we are able to get a better fix on where a sound is coming from, because as our heads move, the sound will get closer or farther from one ear. "But to move, we need a bit of time," says Parra. "If the tone is very short, then we do not have enough time to accumulate information as to which orientation/location is the strongest source of sound."

What's more, Parra says that the 12-kHz sound may not be all that annoying to many adults, because with age there is high-frequency hearing loss, and 12 kHz is too high a tone for many of us to hear.

It's not surprising that the Annoy-a-tron is sold by a company called ThinkGeek, an online site that offers "Stuff for smart masses." Uncle Ted seems to favor this site. He bought several of the Annoy-a-trons, as well as its cousin the Eviltron, which is basically the same thing but has a bigger speaker and makes noises like unidentifiable scratching sounds, a gasping last breath, a sinister child laughing, and an eerie whispering of "Hey, can you hear me?"

The Annoy-a-tron has been a good seller for ThinkGeek. "It's a pretty inexpensive, fun item," says ThinkGeek cofounder Scott Smith. "I think the fun factor to cost ratio is very good. We've gotten a lot of letters from people who put them in coworkers' offices and gotten a lot of entertainment value out of them." Boy, have they gotten letters. Here's one testimonial they've published on their Web site:

> Dear friends at thinkgeek.com,
>
> I recently acquired the "Annoy-A-Tron" from your web site. Actually, I acquired two, thinking that perhaps two devices might be necessary to truly splinter the minds of my friends and co-workers. How woefully did I underestimate this powerful tool.
>
> I have watched this simple device transform a (until-now) mild-mannered colleague into a spitting, cussing, paranoid lunatic.
>
> He has ordered all of the staff he supervises (not a small number) to locate the source of the dreaded

beeping before doing anything else (but since they are in on the prank, they haven't been much help). So he waits, white-knuckles gripping the edge of his desk, anticipating the next beep.

He speculates that "they" might be doing air-quality testing in the building. This beep must be some device in the ducts detecting dangerous levels of asbestos in the air. Or worse. Radon? Aerosolized mercury? Legionella spores?

The beep means something. What does the beep mean? Is it a warning? It sounds urgent, doesn't it? It's telling us to do something. But what? Replace a battery? Call the authorities? Evacuate the premises? Scrub ourselves with disinfectant and put on haz-mat suits and call our families to give them our tearful goodbyes?

I imagine that soon he will begin to take things apart. He will methodically dismantle all of the electrical devices in his office, creating an unusually precise metaphor for what is happening in his psyche.

I am reminded what a thin and fragile thread keeps us attached to sanity. Today, this tiny little device helped me break a co-worker's mind, and I thank you for the sinfully pleasurable schadenfreude.

My best to you,
John
Seattle, WA

Uncle Ted bought the original Annoy-a-tron. ThinkGeek has since released the Annoy-a-tron 2.0. The newer model is slightly larger and has a few more sounds and a volume control. It's also more expensive. How do you take something that already seems perfectly annoying and improve it? And, why would you?

When volunteers join the Park Slope Volunteer Ambulance Corps, many have to be taught how to drive an ambulance in New York City, which includes siren protocols. Dale Garcia, who has been with the PSVAC for eighteen years and is now the executive officer at the corps, says that his training method is fear-based. "I make them terrified to drive, and then I make them drive." It's all about confidence building, he says.

Sirens are an important component of driving an ambulance. In New York City, ambulances are required to turn on their lights and sirens when responding to emergency calls. That also goes for volunteer ambulance drivers, such as those at the Park Slope Corps. It sounds like a reasonable law, but it doesn't always seem that way to Garcia, who dislikes annoying his neighbors with the noise at 4 a.m. when the streets are empty.

One of the few ground rules for using sirens is that if you're going through an intersection, you're instructed to change the siren call. Studies have shown, and common sense confirms, that intersections pose the greatest risk for collisions between EMS vehicles and everything else. The idea is that the change in sound makes the siren harder to ignore. This is a fact that has become so familiar it's easy to lose sight of how astonishing it really is: even an ambulance siren can fade into the background if it's too predictable.

The use of a siren seems to be more an art than a science. In the basement of the corps, Will Tung takes out a marker and draws a diagram of the sirens available to him and his preferred style. "There are three siren tones. The Wail—which is the classic waahh wow waahh wow. The Yelp, which is a faster wail. And the third one—I call it the phaser. It sounds sort of like nails scratching a chalkboard. Each steps up in rapidness. I usually leave it on Wail, and approaching an intersection I go to Yelp and then back to Wail." He pulls out the phaser only for real tough jams.

In addition to being annoying, part of what makes a siren effective is that people recognize it as a siren. There are nationwide standards, set out largely by the Society of Automotive Engineers, that guide siren makers on what frequencies of sound are designated for emergency vehicles. The frequencies haven't changed significantly over the years, according to one siren maker, but siren users have gotten creative.

In one of the corps ambulances, on an industrial block in downtown Brooklyn, Tung demonstrates the sirens. Where the cup holder is in your car, there's the "Whelan" in this ambulance. There's a red switch to turn it on and off and a knob that can be set to T3 (that's the phaser), Yelp, Wail, HF (for handsfree), MAN, PA, and RAD (for radio). There's a button for a synthetic air horn. Fire trucks still have real air horns, Tung says.

Will likes PA for cruising around—"a yelp with a tail," he says. It's what most FDNY EMS drivers use. There are tricks to remixing the sirens. Certain settings allow you to control them with the horn and the megaphone, allowing for maximum siren control. There are ways to get the sirens to cycle automatically or move up in pitch as they go through the calls.

"That gets people to move because it's really annoying," Tung says.

Yet in a city like New York, which not only never sleeps but never really shuts up either, sirens aren't always annoying enough. Dale Garcia and Will Tung agreed that many drivers either don't or can't seem to get out of the way of an ambulance.

Garcia thinks that New Yorkers may be especially good at ignoring things. For example, one bitter cold night on 3rd Avenue and 5th Street in Brooklyn, a car caught on fire. When Garcia arrived, thirty-foot flames were shooting out of the car. Fortunately, there was space around the vehicle, and Garcia parked the ambulance near the car to block off the area and keep people at a safe distance. Then, in what seemed like an (almost) impossible New York minute, a man came up to Garcia's ambulance, knocked on the window, and said, "Could you move your ambulance? I'd like to park my car."

Some of us are better than others at paying attention only to the things we want to pay attention to. The job of an EMS driver—or an Annoy-a-tron designer—is to overcome everyone's ability to ignore things.

David Huron is interested in music and our brains. He's a musicologist and the head of the Cognitive and Systematic Musicology Laboratory in the School of Music at Ohio State University. In studying why humans are so enthusiastic about some sounds, he's turned up a wealth of insights into what makes us so unenthusiastic about others. As the cell phone studies suggest, attention-grabbing noises often provoke the most backlash.

Nature is a good place to look for answers to most questions, including what makes a sound intrinsically annoying.

You're sitting outside on the deck of your house. You've got the newspaper and your morning coffee. A fly comes by and decides that your head is the most interesting and entertaining thing it has ever seen. It never seems to tire of buzzing around and around your ears. It's not deterred by the newspaper, which has now been rolled up for use as a weapon. The swatting seems to add to the fly's thrill. The morning paper and coffee may soothe you, but they're no matches for the fly. There's never a time when a fly buzzing around your head isn't annoying. What accounts for this?

It's partly about the optimism that someday the fly will find someone else's head to circle. It's partly that the exact route the fly takes around your ears is unpredictable. It's partly unpleasant because flies are a little gross—they remind us of dog poop and rotting carcasses. Yet there's something else about flies—the sound their little wings produce is unpleasant.

> Fly: zzzzzzZZZZZZZzzzzzzzz . . .
> You: Maybe it's gone.
> Fly: ZZZZZZZZZ!

Flies are not trying to get your attention; they're born with that ability.

When flies zip to and fro past your ears, the volume of the buzz changes as it moves closer and farther away. This erratic volume change is akin to the concept of roughness. Roughness is the measure of the change in amplitude of a sound vibration over time—the rate at which the sound gets louder and softer. Slow roughness is called beating—you've probably heard it when someone tunes a guitar. Fast roughness melts into a hum. If the roughness is just right, though, it's hard on the ears. "What roughness does is that it actually interferes with the ability of the auditory system to pull information out of the environment," says Huron. His theory is that because roughness makes it hard for us to hear other things, we don't like it. There's a good evolutionary reason not to like rough sounds because they interfere with our ability to perceive other sounds around us, he says. "It's one of the reasons why French people find English annoying. French is not a very highly inflected language. Each of the syllables tends to be equivalent—roughly the same in duration, approximately the same in amplitude or loudness. It sounds a bit like a sewing machine. It's ta tatatata.

"English, by contrast, is a very highly stressed or inflected language," says Huron. "We have weak and strong syllables. It's speech that keeps whacking you over the head, slapping you in the ear. That's related to the experience of roughness. To the French, the classic description of English is that it sounds like a fly buzzing around your head."

As cars become more sound-proof and pedestrians stop up their ears with headphones and cell phones, siren companies are looking for new ways to be heard. Meet the Rumbler. It's the big gun. It doesn't operate like traditional sirens. "It's an auxiliary device, to be used in conjunction with the standard siren products," says Paul Gergets, the director of engineering for mobile systems at Federal Signal, the company that makes the Rumbler. You wouldn't turn on the Rumbler if you were simply responding to a call. It's for tough situations. It's for when the usual sirens don't move people.

You guessed it—the Rumbler's claim to fame is that it rumbles. From the grill of the vehicle, it shoots out a low-frequency sound that is meant to be felt more than heard. Federal Signal describes it this way: "This system provides penetrating/vibrating low-frequency sound waves that allow vehicle operators and nearby pedestrians to feel the sound."

Think of what happens when you're stopped at a red light in front of a car blasting its bass. It shakes the windows and the rear-view mirror. The Rumbler is made to do this to the cars around it.

The Rumbler was born from a request by the Florida Highway Patrol, which was having trouble getting people to move out of the way. The patrol was looking for "a different type of siren tone for instances where they were not getting the attention of people with their standard sirens," says Gergets. "With the regular siren you're competing against stereos, quiet car environments, cell phones, et cetera, and the Rumbler gives you an alternative method for getting someone's attention."

Getting people's attention isn't merely a matter of getting to an emergency more quickly. Sirens protect EMS personnel as well. "I almost get killed one in three times I'm in this thing," Dale says, pointing at a white sedan he drives, which doesn't look much like an emergency vehicle until he revs up the sirens and flicks on the lights. The car is also outfitted with a Rumbler.

You can now find the Rumber installed in police cars across the country, but not everyone likes it. Some are complaining that the Rumbler is frankly too annoying. NoiseOff—"The coalition against noise pollution"—points out on one of its fliers: "The siren can be heard and felt from a distance up to 200 feet away. It easily penetrates into nearby homes and apartments even with windows closed. . . . Its use presents a new form of urban blight where residents are made captive to intense low frequency noise."

This complaint gets to the paradox of good annoyances. Most people would probably agree that a little annoyance from sirens is a small price to pay to live in a society where people can get medical care quickly. Good annoyances are fragile, however—make them a little more annoying and they're no longer good. They're simply annoying.

Imagine a graph with "utility" on one axis and "annoyance" on the other. If you plot something in the high-annoyance, low-utility quadrant, most people would say, "No, thanks." Low annoyance, high utility? "Yes, please." Yet finding the tipping point often isn't a straightforward calculation. Besides, we don't all agree on what's pleasant and what's unpleasant, and sometimes we can't even decide whether one thing is irritating or irresistible.

2

A Case of Mistaken Intensity

Shortly after Christopher Columbus arrived in the Americas, the famous explorer noticed something curious. The natives he encountered tended to cook their food with a spice that Columbus thought tasted terrible. Not only did it taste bad, it set their mouths on fire. Columbus was astounded that people willingly ate this stuff. "All the people will not eat without it, considering it very salutary," he wrote in his diary on January 15, 1493.[1]

The spice was chili pepper. If Columbus was surprised that it was popular with the denizens of the New World in 1493, he'd probably be shocked to learn that the chili pepper has only grown in popularity during the last five centuries. It's estimated that one-third of the planet's population eats chili pepper in one form or another each day.

Why do people enjoy eating something that at least initially tastes bad and even causes pain? And what's this got to do with annoyingness? Good questions, says Paul Rozin, a psychologist at the University of Pennsylvania. With his help, we'll tackle the chili-eating conundrum first.

Rozin likes to study quirky topics. He has devoted much of his career in psychology to discovering why certain things disgust people. He's also interested in the flip side of that: why other things are attractive. His interest in the popularity of chili pepper began in the 1970s.

If you want to study annoyingness, you have to spend a lot of time learning about mildly objectionable things, and chili peppers are right on the border between pleasant and unpleasant. When we describe a food as delicious, we usually mean something that everyone would like. We can all agree that a certain restaurant's french fries are great or an ice cream shop's sundaes are sublime. By contrast, one person's deliciously spicy burrito could be positively inedible to his friends. If you want to figure out what makes something unpleasant, chili peppers are an interesting test case.

Rozin says that there's no question that eating chili peppers is an innately negative experience. "We have all kinds of evidence that little children don't like this taste." In some chili-eating cultures, women rub chili powder on their breasts to speed up the weaning process.

There's a lot of conjecture about why people started to eat chilies in the first place, because evidence has shown that they've been part of the human diet for approximately nine thousand years. Some ethnopharmacologists (yes, there is such a discipline—the field even has its own journal) have suggested that the Maya ate peppers for their antimicrobial properties.[2] More recently, scientists in Canada have shown that despite their potential for setting the lining of your esophagus and stomach on fire, chilies contain a chemical that suppresses the gut bacteria *Helicobacter pylori*.[3] That's a good thing, because *H. pylori* is the bacterium associated with gastric ulcers.

Are people eating chili peppers for their health, then? "I'm not convinced of it," says Rozin. The evidence is circumstantial at best. Presumably, ancient cultures were unaware that the Nobel Prize would be awarded in 2005 for the discovery of the relationship between *H. pylori* and ulcers.

There are other theories about pepper's popularity. "There's the idea that it disguises decay," says Rozin. "People were eating food without refrigerators, and they put this thing on, and they wouldn't notice decay. I don't think that makes a lot of sense."

It's also true that chili peppers contain large amounts of vitamins A and C. "Surely, there are better ways to get your vitamins without having to burn your mouth off," says Rozin.

To learn what was really behind people's passion for peppers, in the late 1970s Rozin and some colleagues visited a village in the Mexican highlands near Oaxaca. Except for the smallest children, nearly everyone in the village ate peppers in one form or another every day, and it clearly was not a case of "Eat your chili or you won't get dessert." To prove this, he conducted a simple experiment.

The local markets sold treats in cellophane packets. The treats came in two varieties: sweet and savory. The sweet kind consisted of sour fruits flavored with sugar. The savory type was ground chili peppers mixed with salt. Rozin bought up the town's supply of these packets—not a major investment, because they were only a penny apiece—and gave children a choice: sweet or savory. Children who were older than five routinely picked the chili-and-salt treat over the sugar-and-fruit one.

Rozin also discovered that people actually like the burning feeling in their mouths that lingers even after the pepper is swallowed. This pleasure appears to be limited to the mouth. No one seems to like the burn of a chili pepper in the eye.

Animals apparently do not experience a similar pleasure from pain. To prove this, Rozin's team offered the pigs and the dogs in the village a choice of a tortilla with hot sauce and a tortilla without. "We did not find a single animal in the village who would take the hot one first," he says.

Many researchers have suggested that the reason people tolerate the chili burn is that they become inured to it, although this doesn't answer the question of why people start to eat chilies in the first place. This is known as the desensitization theory. The chemical that packs the chili's punch is called capsaicin. "It's been known for many years that you can desensitize nerve fibers to capsaicin," says David Julius. In 1997, Julius identified the receptor that responds to capsaicin.

Julius says that with repeated exposure, capsaicin can actually cause damage to the nerve fibers. The damage is reversible, though: the nerve fiber can recover with time. For a certain period of time, however, the nerve is less able to signal to the brain.

Rozin doesn't think that desensitization explains people's chili-eating behavior, either. Yes, he says, there probably is some desensitization taking place, but "there would have to be positive features of chili that support a preference after desensitization; otherwise, desensitization would lead to neutral responses."[4] In other words, desensitization explains only why people can tolerate chilies, not why they actually like to eat them.

There are four lines of experimental evidence to support Rozin's position. In his studies, Rozin has measured the threshold at which people can detect a chili's burning sensation. If the desensitization hypothesis were correct, then people who eat a lot of chilies should have a higher threshold for detecting the burn. So Rozin tested the residents of the Mexican village, who eat a lot of chilies, and compared their thresholds with students at the University of Pennsylvania, who ate far fewer chilies. There was only a tiny difference.

The second line of evidence is that Penn students who like chili peppers should have a higher threshold than students who don't. Again, the difference was marginal.

Third, people who really like chilies should have a higher threshold for detecting the burning sensation, but Rozin showed that there was no relationship between taste preference and threshold.

Finally, if you eat chilies every day of your life, your threshold should get higher with age—but it doesn't.

Rozin believes that the solution to the chili mystery is what he calls hedonic reversal. Something that tastes terrible when you first eat it over time becomes a delightful taste. "It's something in your brain that's switched from a negative evaluation to a positive evaluation," he says.

This does not happen only with chilies. Rozin attributes it to a more general phenomenon known as benign masochism. We like to do things that are innately negative. For example, says Rozin, people like to go to sad movies, even though they make us cry. People like disgusting jokes, even though these are, well, disgusting. Some people even like pain. For certain people, pain and pleasure have a long history of coexisting.

"What kind of crazy species are we?" asks Rozin. For example, people actually line up and pay money to have the wits scared out of them on a roller coaster. "Can you imagine a dog going on a roller coaster and paying for a second ride? We are the only species, as far as I know, to seek out innately negative events."

Although Rozin is certain that the phenomenon of hedonic reversal is real, he's less certain about why it happens. He does have a theory. "People get pleasure out of the fact that their bodies are telling them something that they know is not the case," he says. So, on a roller coaster you can be excited, even titillated by the fear, because you know you're not really threatened. "In a sad movie, you're crying and enjoying it because it's not really sad. Your body is being tricked into feeling it's sad, but you know it's not really happening. That sort of disparity becomes a source of pleasure, but only for humans."

If you're a fan of chili peppers, you might be thinking it's simpler than this: they taste good. In fact, you may have a brand preference when it comes to hot sauce or a favorite variety of spicy peppers, which would seem to point to flavor as a key factor. The innately negative part, the burning of your tongue, may not have much of an attraction for you at all.

Michael Cunningham, a professor of psychology and communication at the University of Louisville in Kentucky, agrees with you. "Hedonic reversals are tricky," he says. "I think there is a combination of positive emotion mixed in with the negative."

Take roller coasters. "With roller coasters, you get the vistas," he says. "You get the sensation of speed. I don't know whether the predominant reaction is one of fear. I think it's exhilaration, with a little bit of fear thrown in." Besides, for some people there's a kind of joy that accompanies an adrenaline rush.

Cunningham also sees a positive side to sadness. "Sadness is nature's way of putting things in perspective," he says. "You slow down your rate of thinking, and you do some reevaluating, so it can have a positive aspect to it."

As for chili peppers, Cunningham says that even with scalding-hot chili peppers, it's not simply about pain. A pleasurable taste exists in there somewhere; otherwise, people wouldn't be eating them. "People don't just drip sulfuric acid on their tongues," he says. "At least, I'm not aware of any people who do."

It's possible that the principle behind hedonic reversal is a variation of the phenomenon known as "runner's high." Certain chemicals produced by the brain act the way that morphine and other opioid painkillers do. Studies show that the body produces these chemicals in greater numbers after a long run, but they may also be created in response to painful or even strongly emotional experiences. Perhaps hedonic reversal is a shortcut to running a marathon. Or maybe it's related to that joke about the man who is seen banging his head against a wall. When asked why he is doing this, he replies, "Because it feels so good when I stop."

Hedonic reversal does not apply universally. "Nausea is one of the few negative sensations that I think nobody enjoys," says Rozin, although he's not exactly sure why. One possibility is that nausea is inevitably caused by, or followed by, something truly bad. "It's very difficult to be nauseous and not have something wrong," says Rozin. "You can feel pain, as in a massage, and not really have anything wrong with your body. Nausea is a pretty reliable symptom of something going wrong."

Yale psychologist Paul Bloom agrees with Rozin that part of the pleasure of painful stimuli is that as long as it is safe—that is, as long as a movie or a chili pepper doesn't actually endanger us—then we can enjoy it. Yet horror movies and hot peppers evoke strong sensations, just as love stories do. Perhaps the reversal works only if there is some distance between our normal, resting state and the intensity of the emotion. Maybe this is why annoyances are not really susceptible to hedonic reversal. By their nature, annoyances are minor. What fun is it to experience a minor annoyance? It would be akin to the fun of eating bland food. In fact, there's a famous Mel Brooks quote along these lines: "I cut my finger. That's tragedy. A man walks into an open sewer and dies. *That's* comedy."

If annoyances are mild, though, how is mildness measured? How much is too much? For any field of scientific endeavor, taking measurements is key. How hard is a particular mineral?

At what temperature does a compound freeze? How much carbon dioxide is being released into the atmosphere? What is the red shift of a particular quasar? How long does it take a rat to complete a maze? Accurate measurements are essential to the progress of science.

One of the biggest challenges facing a new scientific field, such as the study of annoyance, is that it has to develop the instruments to take measurements. There are no annoyingometers (although most people do come equipped with annoydar) and no well-validated personality inventories. Clearly, if progress is to be made in understanding why certain things or people are so irritating, scientists will need ways to answer two kinds of questions: how annoying someone or something is, and how much someone is annoyed by things or people in his or her environment.

Linda Bartoshuk is interested in the latter question. She is a psychology professor at the University of Florida and is in demand as a speaker at meetings around the world. She has also been president of the Association for Psychological Science and a member of the National Academy of Sciences, both organizations with Washington, D.C., headquarters. She travels frequently between Gainesville and Washington.

To fly from Gainesville to Washington, you have to stop in Charlotte, and from painful experience she knows that catching a tight connection in Charlotte rarely works. "The flight from Gainesville is always late," she explains. It's annoying but so predictable that she's only mildly irritated by it.

Bartoshuk is with the Center for Taste and Smell at the University of Florida. She has spent a substantial part of her career studying how people taste things. In the 1980s, she discovered a group of people whom she dubbed supertasters.

These are individuals who are much more sensitive than most people to food flavors. Foods that are only somewhat bitter to "normal" tasters are unbearably bitter to supertasters. The discovery of supertasters underscored a problem that she has focused on for the last decade: how to measure something subjective such as taste in a way that you can make meaningful comparisons between two people. What does it mean to say something is "very salty" or "sort of sweet" or "slightly bitter?" You know what *you* mean when you say that, but it means something very different if you happen to be a supertaster.

Taste belongs to a class of experiences known as hedonic experiences. In general, these are qualities that you can sense or feel but can't really measure in a physical way. For example, a food chemist can tell you the amount of sodium chloride in a particular food, and yes, the saltiness of food depends on the amount of sodium chloride in it. Yet a McDonald's Vanilla Triple Shake in a twenty-one-ounce cup has more sodium than a medium order of french fries, and although you may have criticisms about the McDonald's Vanilla Triple Shake, "too salty" is not likely to be one of them.[5]

Plenty of other experiences only partly depend on physical measurements. The loudness of sound, the brightness of light, and the degree that you're in love can all be rated on a 9-point scale, where 1 is the least and 9 is the strongest, but is the "9" of men the same as the "9" of women when it comes to love? Some people would say no.

Pain can also be considered a hedonic experience. Yes, you can measure the amount of force that is applied to your thumb when you accidentally miss the nail with your hammer. And yes, if you're asked, "On a scale of 1 to 9, how much pain are you in?" you might say 9. How does that 9 compare with the 9 that many women experience when they give birth?

The traditional scales work on an individual basis. Hospitals routinely ask patients to rate how much pain they are in, on a 1-to-9 scale, to determine whether to administer an analgesic. If your pain is 7, and you take Tylenol with codeine, and your pain drops to a 3, that's a meaningful measurement.

Problems arise, however, when people try to make comparisons. Bartoshuk's research suggests that women's pain tolerance, in absolute terms, is higher than men's, probably because men don't experience anything quite as painful as childbirth. This means that if 4 is the magic number for receiving an analgesic in the hospital, women will actually have to experience more pain before they qualify to have their pain relieved.

Now, Bartoshuk has begun to think about how we can measure annoyance. Measuring annoyances poses the same kind of problems as measuring pain or love or taste. "I was thinking about that when I changed planes in Charlotte," says Bartoshuk, when she stopped for a bite of lunch at National Airport before heading to downtown Washington for a meeting. "While we were waiting to board the flight to Washington, I asked the woman standing next to me, 'Do you get more annoyed by some things than others?'"

Not surprisingly, the woman said yes. Bartoshuk says she asked because she wanted to double-check her belief that the sensation of annoyance has a range of intensities. Clearly, it does. Some things are more annoying than others. That's an important property of the experience of being annoyed. "And then I said to her, 'Think of the most angry you've ever been in your life and think of the most annoyed. Which was more intense?' 'Anger, definitely,' the woman said." Bartoshuk says those two properties, a varying intensity and an ability to compare annoyance with another sensation, such as anger, will help her develop a scale for annoyance. That's what she is planning to do.

Why develop an annoying scale? "Because annoyance is also a hedonic experience," she thinks. This means it can be measured to make comparisons between groups of people. Bartoshuk's basic approach is to try to anchor a hedonic scale to something that is actually measurable. For example, she will ask people what is the brightest light they've ever seen. Most people will say the light coming from the sun. That's something that can be measured physically, and it's the same for everyone in the world.

Then she'll ask people how the happiest they've ever been compares with the brightest light they've ever seen on a scale from 1 to 100. It's a way to anchor the happy score. This may seem odd, but remember, they're being asked to compare something that is inherently subjective with something that is essentially objective: the light from the sun. If your happiest feeling is only a 65 on the sun scale and mine is 95 on the sun scale, then my happiest is more intense than yours. To compare our happiness, our subjective ratings need to be adjusted.

If she tests a hundred people, she can then compare men's happiness scores with women's happiness scores because they are all anchored by the sunlight standard. Or she can measure whether obese people are happier than lean people. The comparisons become meaningful because of the absolute standard they're measured against.

•   •   •

Another type of scaling method that Bartoshuk is experiment-ing with involves training the subjects in her studies to com-pare food taste sensations with the loudness of sounds. She told them, "If you give a sound a 9 on a scale of 0 to 9, and you give a food a 9, it means the intensity of liking the food is equal to the intensity of the loudness." Similarly, if you were indifferent to a food, this would be linked to a barely audible sound.

At first, many subjects think that comparing loudness with taste is daft, but Bartoshuk has an easy way to show them that at least in principle, it's possible. She gives them a small sip of water that has a barely detectable amount of salt in it, and then she plays them a sound so loud it makes their teeth rattle. "And I ask, 'Do they match?' And they say, 'Of course, they don't.' Then I give them a sip of extremely salty water and play an extremely soft tone, and I ask, 'Do they match?' And they say, 'No.' So, they understand that you can match these up."

Sounds can be measured with well-calibrated instruments. If you can get people to anchor their likeness scale to a sound scale, where 1 is the softest sound they can possibly hear and 10 is the loudest sound they can possibly stand, then you can start to say meaningful things about how a 5 on one person's likeness scale compares with a 5 on someone else's likeness scale.

To set up her test of annoyance, Bartoshuk piggybacked it onto another experiment she's working on. She has teamed up with plant biologist Harry Klee to try to measure what people like about tomatoes. In particular, she wants to help Klee design a tomato variety that yields many fruits, some-thing that farmers like, and is good tasting, something that consumers like.

In this particular case, after collecting information about age, weight, sex, and a few other demographic variables, Bartoshuk asks subjects to think of the one thing that gave them the most pleasure and assign that a score of 100. By the way, most people do not assign 100 to sex. It's usually something more along the lines of being with a loved one or creating something special. Then she asks her subjects to give a score of minus 100 to the most unpleasant experience they've ever had. This might be death of a loved one, a really painful injury, or the pain of childbirth. Then she asks them to assign a score to questions such as, How much do you like your favorite food? What's the most amused you've ever been? What's the best lecture you've ever heard (these are largely college students)? And, What's the best tomato you've ever eaten? Finally, she asks them to assign a score to the most annoyed they've ever been and the most angry they've ever been.

The preliminary results were gratifying. "It's clear that the distributions of ratings of annoyance and anger are quite different," says Bartoshuk. "That is probably enough to argue that annoyance is not a subset of anger."

In general, women rated the most annoyed they'd ever been as less intense than men's ratings. Perhaps more surprising was the relationship between body mass index and annoyance. Bartoshuk found that overweight people tended to be more annoyed than normal or underweight people were, although it will require more study participants to be certain that this is a real difference.

Perhaps most interesting for Bartoshuk: supertasters have more intense maximum anger and annoyance. This suggests that supertasters are also superfeelers. This last point could become extremely important. Bartoshuk is toying with the notion that the same absolute standard that determines whether someone is a supertaster could be used to compare people's experience of how annoying something is.

Here's how it would work. You can determine with virtual certainty whether people are supertasters by counting how many fungiform papillae are present on their tongues. These papillae contain our taste buds, structures that turn the chemical constituents of food into signals that our nerves can carry to our brains. The more you have, the more sensitive you are to tastes. Because the number of fungiform papillae is measurable, just as the number of photons coming from the sun is measurable, Bartoshuk hopes she can prove that the papillae count will be her Rosetta stone for scaling sensations such as annoyance. Ultimately, she wants scientists to get out of the annoying habit of using scales that can't be compared.

While Bartoshuk is trying to understand how intensely people feel annoyance, other researchers are trying to figure *what* provokes the most intensely annoying feelings—and why.

3

Fingernails on a Chalkboard

Randolph Blake is a vision specialist. He has studied the intersection of psychology and sight for most of his career. Now a professor of psychology at Vanderbilt University, he's interested in figuring out which parts of the brain process various kinds of visual information.

Back in 1986, Blake was working on the infant science of image processing. Forget about automatic red-eye reduction; the world hadn't even been introduced to Photoshop yet (it was released in 1990). Manipulating a digital image meant writing your own computer program to do it. To test his programming approach, Blake started with sound because, like light, it's made up of complex waveforms that vary in frequency and amplitude—but it's simpler and easier to analyze.

Blake chose to analyze annoying sounds. He was curious whether certain frequencies are intrinsically annoying to us. Almost any sound can be annoying if it is blasted at an ear-splitting level. Certain sounds, however—even at low levels—have a reputation for provoking instant annoyance. Perhaps most infamously, there is the sound of fingernails on a chalkboard. Blake wondered, What makes this sound unpleasant to so many people?

Step one: Create a device that consistently produces the fingernails-on-a-chalkboard sound and confirm that people find the noise exceptionally annoying. "I went to an Ace hardware store and got a three-pronged garden tool and a piece of slate," Blake says. It turns that out when you slowly scrape the True Value Pacemaker cultivator over a slate surface, the sound produced is "disturbingly similar to the sound of fingernails scratching across a chalkboard," Blake and his colleagues wrote in the journal *Perception and Psychophysics*.[1]

The researchers recorded the synthetic fingernail sound in the auditory labs at Northwestern University, the institution where Blake worked at the time, with a Teac A-3300S reel-to-reel tape recorder (it's 1986, remember) and an AKG Acoustics CK 4 microphone. They also catalogued a few other irritating noises. They rubbed two pieces of Styrofoam together. They shook metal parts. They dragged a stool across the floor. They ran a blender. They opened a squeaky metal drawer, over and over again. "I have to admit, you can immunize yourself," says Blake. "If you listened to these sounds over and over—as I had to do while I was preparing for this study—they never lost their aversive quality, but the valence of the experience was toned down a little bit." Total immunity wasn't possible. "Even to this day," he says, "if you mention fingernails scraping on a chalkboard, I get chills just thinking about it."

Step two: Find people to listen to these sounds ("They weren't coerced," Blake insists) and have them rank the sounds according to their annoyingness. A session took about twenty to thirty minutes. Then the participants were asked to rate the sounds somewhere on a scale between pleasant and unpleasant.

Chimes were the most popular sound, but this isn't exactly a ringing endorsement, given the competition. On the other end of the spectrum, the participants were highly unenthusiastic about the sounds of scraping wood and Styrofoam rubbing. The champion of the unpleasant category, however, was the fingernails-on-chalkboard sound of the garden tool running across slate.

The full ranking of sounds from pleasant to unpleasant is as follows:

1. Chimes
2. Rotating bicycle tire
3. Running water
4. Jingling keys
5. Pure tone
6. Pencil sharpener
7. Shaking metal parts
8. White noise
9. Compressed air
10. Blender motor
11. Dragged stool

12. Metal drawer being opened
13. Scraping wood
14. Scraping metal
15. Rubbing two pieces of Styrofoam together
16. Scraping slate [with a garden tool]

Step three: Analyze the acoustic properties of the fingernail scrape to look for acoustic signatures that could explain
the essence of its annoyingness.

Sound is simply a change in pressure over time. The bigger
the change in pressure, the louder the sound. When the metal
prongs of the garden tool are dragged across a piece of slate,
the friction between the two surfaces causes vibrations. These
vibrations are changes in pressure. The frequency of a sound
corresponds to how many pressure changes occur during the
course of a second. The higher the frequency, the more pressure oscillations per second; the lower, the fewer. We hear
higher frequencies as higher pitches.

A sound, however, is more than the sum of its vibrations. Blake says that if you just mix the frequency components randomly, you get noise—like the hissing of a radio
between signals. All of the frequencies that are present in the
fingernails-on-a-chalkboard sound might be present in static,
Blake says, but they aren't arranged in the same way. What
gives a creak, a squawk, or a squeal its signature is how the
peaks and troughs of the component sound waves appear in
relation to one another over time.

Think of it like cooking: the proportions of the ingredients
and when they're added can mean the difference between

marinara sauce and a Bloody Mary. The same is metaphorically true for sounds, with the frequencies as the ingredients.

The question Blake was trying to get at was: What frequencies were poisoning the pot? Signal processing helps answer this question by providing the recipe for the sound, revealing the mixture of component frequencies and at what levels they are added.

To try to understand which frequencies were the offending ones, the researchers tried removing ingredients. They wondered, At what point when we remove certain frequencies does the sound lose its aversive quality?

Blake hypothesized that the high frequencies were the root of the problem. Think about how you might describe the fingernail-scraping sound. The adjectives that come to mind are *shrill*, *piercing*, *sharp*. They're pejorative, and they suggest that the offensive parts are the high pitches. "Intuition told us that if we removed the really high frequencies, that would de-fang the noise," Blake says.

The researchers were wrong. Blake filtered out the high pitches and—weirdly—the sound was still really annoying. The sound was different: it was more muffled but not more pleasant, according to the study subjects.

It turned out that the sound got less annoying to the listeners only when the middle-range frequencies were taken out. The annoying frequencies were the mundane 500 to 2,000 Hz (Hz, or hertz, is the scientific unit for frequency, or in this case, pressure variations per second). These frequencies are right in the middle of our hearing range: humans can hear frequencies from about 20 Hz to 20,000 Hz—and that upper limit drops as our ears age.[2]

All ears basically work the same way: think of them as funnels. Sound waves (pressure oscillations) travel through the air, shoot down the ear canal, and get absorbed by the eardrum, a membrane gate at the end of the ear canal. The vibrations travel through tiny bones that connect the eardrum to the cochlea—a hollow tube that is sort of like a snail shell. "If you were to unravel the snail, it's essentially this long tube that's divided by a membrane," says Josh McDermott, a neuroscientist at New York University. "Different parts of the tube are sensitive to different frequencies. The part closest to the eardrum is sensitive to high frequencies and the part that's farthest away is sensitive to low frequencies."

So far, everything is mechanical: pressure oscillations are jiggling a membrane in your ear. Enter hair cells. The membrane is coated with them. These receptors get their name because they have little organelles that stick out from the cell wall like cowlicks. They're called stereocilia and they're small—about 5 microns long, one-twentieth the width of a human hair. Small but important: the stereocilia are responsible for detecting the jiggling. The hair cells do the remarkable task of translating those physical signals into electrical pulses that are sent to the brain. After the hair cells translate the pressure oscillations into electrical signals, the signals are transmitted to subcortical regions in the mid-brain, and then they make their way to the thalamus and the cortex, "and then a lot of stuff happens that we don't understand," McDermott says.

Not all sounds are heard equally: the human ear seems to have preferences for certain frequencies. The frequencies that contribute most to the annoyingness of the scraping sound are on the low end of the frequency range that our ear is most sensitive to. Humans can detect frequencies between

2,000 Hz and 5,000 Hz at lower volumes than other sounds. Around 3,000 Hz also happens to be the natural resonant frequency of the ear canal, studies show. This means that when a 3,000-Hz signal goes into the ear, it's naturally amplified, due to the shape of the ear canal.[3]

"It means that you can hear a sound at 3,000 Hz that has much less than a quarter of the energy of a sound at, say, 1,000 Hz," says David Huron. "Here's what's fun. We record a bunch of different sounds made by humans, and we find out which sound has the most amount of energy right around 3,000 Hz that humans make. The answer is a scream. This is true of males, females, and children. When men scream, they break into a falsetto. They end up producing the max amount of energy in the same region as women and children when they scream. What this means is that the sound that we can detect at the greatest distance is the human scream. We're most sensitive to a human scream." Sounds in this frequency range will "distract you from any other task you're involved in," says Huron. This may explain why the fingernail noise got less annoying when the middle frequencies were removed—when the energies we're most sensitive to are removed from the noise, it's easier to tune out.

The 2,000 to 5,000 Hz range is also where the ear is most vulnerable, McDermott says. "If someone listens to lots of loud sounds, and you look at where they have hearing loss, it's usually going to be in that range. At least, that's the first place where people have problems." He adds that it's possible that our aversion to those frequencies could be a protective response. Ear preservation is one hypothesis to explain why the fingernails-on-a-chalkboard screech makes us cringe. A sensible way to protect our hearing is to evolve an aversion to sounds that are damaging.

Randolph Blake proposed another hypothesis. Some sounds remind us of something we don't like, which seems to partly explain the annoyance factor.

If you are sensitive to noise annoyances, take heart in the fact that few people are immune, including the most controlled among us. Recall, for example, an anecdote related by Mark Leibovich in January 2009 in the *New York Times*:

> Barack Obama was meeting this month with House Speaker Nancy Pelosi and other lawmakers when Rahm Emanuel, his chief of staff, began nervously cracking a knuckle. Obama turned to complain to Emanuel about his noisy habit. At which point, Emanuel held the offending knuckle up to Obama's left ear and—like an annoying little brother—snapped off a few special cracks.[4]

Knuckle cracking is annoying, even to presidents—but why? Here are a few theories. First, bodily noises annoy us. "The disgust reaction is universal," says Trevor Cox, an acoustician at Salford University's Acoustic Research Centre who has been hunting for the worst sound in the world through his Web-research project BadVibes. Cox posted a variety of sounds on the Internet and asked people to rank them in terms of how bad they were. Nearly half a million votes were tallied, and a gross body sound was the biggest loser: vomiting came in first for the worst sound in the world. (If you remember, earlier we concluded that nothing good ever comes from being nauseated. Vomiting is what we meant when we said, "Nothing good.")

There are intuitive reasons that humans would dislike the sound of vomiting. "There's a whole class of sounds that are annoying because they have certain bodily associations," says David Huron. "There are excellent reasons why listening to the sound of someone retching or anything associated with illness should make us wary of these sounds or find them not very pleasant." Maybe we don't like disgusting sounds as a defense mechanism. It's possible we're programmed to avoid things that can make us sick because that helps us survive. Knuckle cracking isn't a contagious disease, but it may piggyback onto our aversion to other bodily noises.

When Emanuel cracks his knuckle right in the president's ear, part of what makes that annoying is that Emanuel is trying to be annoying. "The intentionality behind a sound will also have a dramatic impact," Huron says. The intent of the noisemaker seems to add or subtract to a noise's annoyance level. Huron calls this a "cognitive overlay." It's the part of the signal analysis that goes beyond "What is this?" and into "How does this make you feel?"

"Why would Rahm want to annoy me? What's wrong with Rahm that he feels the need to do this in public? Why would I select a chief of staff who feels the need to try to subvert me? Why do I feel subverted by knuckle cracking?" Those types of cognitive overlays might have amplified the president's annoyance.

These swirls of thoughts can transform a neutral sound—a barely audible pop—into an unpleasant one.

Fingernails on a chalkboard seem to work without any cognitive overlays. Why does this sound get an instantly negative response from most people? Like retching, fingernails on a chalkboard may remind us of something bad; we're simply not conscious of it.

"The automatic, almost visceral reaction to this sound makes us wonder whether it mimics some naturally occurring, innately aversive event," Blake and his colleagues wrote. The researchers went to the library and thumbed through books filled with pictures of frequency analyses of sounds to see whether any looked like the pictures that Blake generated of the scraping sound. "One that jumped out to us was primate warning cries," Blake says.

Specifically, the garden tool being scraped across slate looked a lot like the cries that some species of monkeys make to signal a predator.

Blake wondered—although he and his colleagues couldn't prove it—whether the widespread aversive reaction to fingernails on a chalkboard is evolutionary, a holdover from the days when a primate screech meant serious trouble. "Regardless of this auditory event's original functional significance, the human brain obviously still registers a strong vestigial response to this chilling sound," the researchers concluded.

How did the research community react to the suggestion that the sound of fingernails on a chalkboard activates an evolutionarily encoded primal fear? "They largely ignored it," Blake says. Yet it caught some people's attention. In 2006, two decades after being published, the paper received its due.[5] Blake and his coauthors were awarded an Ig Nobel Prize, honoring science's strangest discoveries.

•   •   •

Making a credible observation is easier than proving why something is the way it is. Knowing *why* requires mountains of data, replicated by study after study. This is how hypotheses grow into theories. Who knows if our reaction to fingernails on a chalkboard has anything to do with primate warning calls or ear preservation or neither? There haven't been that many investigations into this mystery, but the question hasn't died out, either.

Cotton-top tamarins (*Saguinus oedipus*) are strange-looking primates. The tamarin has a flat face (imagine a pug-monkey cross) and a fan of white hair sticking out of its head. Tamarins are small, weighing only a pound or so on average. They walk on all fours and hail from the Amazon. And they don't listen to music. That was key for Josh McDermott's study. Now a neuroscientist at New York University, McDermott studies music. He's broadly interested in why we like certain types of music: Is there a biological component? Do monkeys show the same preferences?

"Of course, with a monkey you can't just ask them whether they like something," McDermott says. "You have to come up with another method to measure that." The solution was a maze. While he was at Harvard, McDermott and his colleagues built a V-shaped wooden frame with two branches. A speaker was placed at the end of each branch. The monkey is free to run around. When the tamarin is in the left branch of the maze, the left speaker plays one sound. When the monkey moves over to the right branch, the left speaker turns off and the right speaker turns on with a different sound. "The idea was that the animal controlled what it heard by virtue of its position in this maze," McDermott says. No food treats were given. The only reward was a change in sound.

The point of McDermott's study was to ask whether monkeys show a preference for consonant chords over dissonant chords. Consonance is derived from the Latin *com*, "with," and *sonare*, "to sound," and is often described as having a stable feeling; dissonance, the opposite. In Western music, dissonant chords signal pain, grief, and conflict. Think of it like this: most dance music is consonant and most blues songs mildly dissonant. Early Beatles, mostly consonant. Late Beatles, more dissonant. Heavy metal is probably the most dissonant music you've ever heard.

One side of the maze piped out two-note consonant chords: an octave, "c" and "c"; a fifth, "c" and "g", for example; a fourth, "c" and "f." The other side played dissonant chords—minor seconds, tritones, and minor ninths. The monkeys showed no preferences between consonant and dissonant chords. Harvard undergrads, on the other hand, showed a clear preference for consonant sounds.

Even though the purpose of the experiment was to learn about music, McDermott was also curious whether tamarins would show a preference against the sound of fingernails on a chalkboard. He played the sound of fingernails on one branch and white noise from the other branch.

The cotton-top tamarins showed no significant preference for the white noise versus the scraping. They did, however, when given a volume option, choose to spend more time on the side of the maze with lower-volume white noise compared with higher-volume white noise.

This finding tempers Blake's primate warning call theory. The tamarins didn't seem to dislike the fingernail sound—

meaning, at least, that these primates didn't show a preference against it. McDermott offers another explanation for why we don't like the sound of fingernails on a chalkboard. It's rough on the ears. Roughness—remember from the buzzing fly or abrupt English elocution—is a technical term in acoustics that has to do with the amount of volume, or amplitude, modulation per second.

If you were to watch fingernails or garden tools running down slate with a high-speed camera, says David Huron, you would understand. "Your fingernail is grabbing the surface and then as you continue to move your hand down, it's stuck to the board, and then all of a sudden it will slip and jump to the next position." It's called, Huron says, a "stick-slip sound production." This produces a highly unpredictable, varied sound. "You get periods where it almost sounds like a whistle. And then there are periods where it becomes very rough— and those are the ones that tend to make people cringe the most," says Josh McDermott.

Guitar players know roughness as beating. When you tune a guitar, you typically fret a string on its fifth fret and play the next string down. When the two notes are slightly out of tune, you hear the volume go up and down—kind of like wowuuuwowuuu. Those are the individual peaks and valleys in the waveform. The beating slows as the pitches approach each other and stops when the two pitches are perfectly in synch. "People don't usually call that rough," McDermott says. "Those are just beats." As the pitches move farther apart, the beat frequency increases, and the sound will start to sound rough. When the notes are more than 20 Hz apart in frequency, McDermott says, you can't hear the wowuuuwowuuu, and that's roughness. Then when the beating goes up to 75 to

100 Hz, the roughness goes away—it's too fast to resolve as rough.

Roughness has been scientifically proved to be annoying.[6] Car manufacturers, for instance, have done many studies on how to minimize annoying sounds generated by cars. "One of the biggest factors determining whether a sound will be annoying or not annoying is how smooth the amplitude envelope is," McDermott says. The envelope is the shape of the amplitude of a sound over time. A rough envelope doesn't look much like an envelope at all. It looks more like an accordion. If it has that accordion shape—if the volume goes up and down rapidly—the sound tends to annoy people. This might be a factor in why the fingernails-on-chalkboard sound is so annoying: it's quite rough.

As for why we don't like roughness, there's no clear answer. McDermott says, "It's a bit harder to say why sound roughness is considered unpleasant—as far as we know, it is not harmful to the ears." David Huron suggests that we don't like it because rough sounds interfere with our ability to hear, to pull information out of the environment.

The fingernail mystery remains unsolved—but the leads are helpful. Distracting, rough, ear preservation, adapted aversion: these are some of the theories for what makes certain sounds intrinsically unpleasant—explaining their widespread ability to annoy.

4

Skunked

Smells may be the sneakiest of all annoyances. They're invisible. They're silent. You are aware of them only after it's too late. And they're powerful. Pleasant smells can transport you instantly to a memory of your grandmother's kitchen or your favorite swimming hole. Unfortunately, unpleasant ones have the same effect.

When you consider that a ten-pound fur ball can ward off a nine-hundred-pound bear simply by suggesting that a bad smell is coming, you realize how powerful odors can be. Think of that for a moment. A porcupine went to the trouble of evolving a coat of razor-sharp spines, and that's not as effective as a skunk's primary weapon. Skunks command the forest through smelliness. The aerosol spray isn't deadly, it's annoying. It's so annoying that it can repel almost everything, including much bigger, stronger, and faster predators. For skunks, being annoying means staying alive.

And skunks are deeply annoying. This is clear if you've ever had a dog get sprayed by a skunk. It smells terrible—obviously—and before you can bathe your dog, the scent will seemingly have penetrated every object in your house. Even professional groomers can't completely eliminate the stink from a dog's coat. Every time you think the odor is gone, it reappears. For days, when you (not your dog) go out wearing clothes that were never anywhere near the skunk or the dog, people will say, "Do you smell a skunk? I thought I caught just the faintest whiff of a skunk in here."

Skunk spray looks sort of like pizza grease. It's oily and an orange-yellow color. Skunks produce the spray in their anal glands and turn it into a weapon by shooting it in the direction of predators. Other carnivores, including ferrets, polecats, minks, and weasels, also have the odiferous oil, "but they don't have the ability to aim and squirt it as skunks do," says skunk expert Jerry Dragoo.

Skunks have even evolved special anal nipples for spraying! When a skunk feels threatened, "he's going to aim those nipples, and it's going to come out like a squirt gun," says Dragoo, who has been squirted many times in the course of his career as a mephitologist. The term refers to the study of the family *Mephitidae*, of which skunks are the only members.

Dragoo says that even skunks appear to dislike the odor of skunk spray. This stink also poses a problem for anyone who thinks of becoming a mephitologist. Dragoo says that he can't smell skunk spray, which may explain his career choice.

William Wood, one of the few chemists brave enough to study skunk spray, suggests that the annoying odor may be responsible for slow advances in the field of skunk spray research. In an article called "The History of Skunk Defensive Secretion Research," published in the *Chemical Educator*, Wood wrote, "Skunks and their defensive secretion have both fascinated and repelled natural product chemists. The chemicals secreted by the members of the *mephatinae*, a New World subfamily of the weasel family (*Mustelidae*), are so obnoxious that few chemists have been willing to work with them."[1]

Even if researchers are willing to put up with the odor, their colleagues and neighbors may not be. German scientist and skunk spray pioneer Dr. O. Löw was on an expedition through Texas in the 1870s. He wrote in a letter, "I had frequent opportunity to collect a sufficient quantity of this secretion to establish its chemical constitution, but all my companions protested against it, declaring the odour which clung to me to be unbearable. On my return to New York City I started a few chemical tests, with the little I had collected, when the whole college rose in revolt, shouting, 'A skunk, a skunk is here!' I had to abandon the investigation."

Even in this golden age of fume hoods, studying skunk spray is difficult to do without annoying your colleagues. Wood, of Humboldt State University, was trying to figure out the chemical constituents of skunk spray. That meant collecting samples. "I found dead skunks on the road, and then I put a needle into the duct that had the chemical and pulled it out with a syringe," he says dryly. "Once you've taken a little bit out, the dead skunk would then smell. I would put it in a plastic bag and throw it out the window and then go outside and get it so I wouldn't smell up the building."

The fume hood—which is sort of like an oven fan that sucks air out of an enclosed lab bench—worked great at keeping his room odor-free. The problem is that the contaminated air had to go somewhere. It's usually evacuated from out of the top of the building. This is how Wood discovered who on campus was downwind from him. "The president called me up and said, 'Are you working with skunks today?' So I stopped working on skunks at the university."

Wood started to study skunks because he was interested in chemical ecology: the study of how chemicals carry messages in nature. He says that the field got off the ground about thirty-five years ago, with the study of pheromones—chemical signals that organisms use for communication. Wood has done field research in Africa on the way ticks and tsetse flies use chemicals to communicate; he's also studied ants in Costa Rica. When he was a postdoc at Cornell University, however, he became attracted to the stench of skunks. "Skunks have the obvious chemical defense that everybody knows about, so I worked on those," Wood says.

The spray of the striped skunk (*Mephitis mephitis*) has about seven volatile odor compounds, Wood found. The exact chemical makeup of skunk spray varies from species to species. In all cases, though, the stink is caused by sulfur-laden molecules called thiols. These chemicals, which used to be called mercaptans because of their reactivity with mercury, share similarities in chemical structure to hydrogen sulfide— a toxic compound responsible for the stench of rotten eggs, salt marshes, and bad breath.

Hydrogen sulfide has one sulfur atom and two hydrogen atoms (H_2S). If you remove a hydrogen atom and replace it with a carbon one, then you have a thiol. The length of the carbon chain determines the identity of the thiol: "If you get a thiol on a carbon chain that's about eight carbons long, it no longer has any odor. It has to be a very short-chain thiol [to smell]," Wood says. Methanethiol is the simplest thiol, with only one carbon (e.g., CH_3SH). "Methanethiol and related compounds are produced by the decay of living material," says chemist Eric Block, of the State University of New York at Albany and author of *Garlic and Other Alliums: The Lore and The Science*.[2] "Methanethiol has a horrible, stinky, skunky odor to it."

Just what makes an odor skunky or sweet is mysterious, though. Here's some of what we know about the act of smelling. A molecule floating through the air gets sucked through our nostrils and travels north about seven centimeters until it reaches a ridged tissue called the olfactory epithelium. In that membrane, twenty million olfactory receptors serve as the landing pad for odors. Roughly speaking, an odor molecule locks into a receptor, triggering the nerve to send a signal to the brain.

The most widespread theory for how we detect various odors (and humans are thought to be able to smell about ten thousand different smells) is that receptors have different shapes, and various odor molecules therefore lock into different receptors. Rachel Herz, a psychologist specializing in smell at Brown University, wrote, "Different scents activate different arrays of olfactory receptors in the olfactory epithelia, producing specific firing patterns of neurons in the olfactory bulb. The specific pattern of electrical activity in the olfactory bulb then determines the scent we perceive. The scent of a mango elicits a different pattern of neural impulses than the smell of a skunk." That's a description from her book *The Scent of Desire*.[3] Then our brains translate these patterns into "skunk spray, yuck" or "mango, yum."

That's a broad-stroke picture of scent perception, but what drives our preferences for certain odors is perhaps more contentious. When it comes to our widespread dislike of skunk spray, Wood and Block theorize that our aversion to these molecules may be protective, something skunks have taken advantage of.

"Thiols and certain nitrogen compounds are intimately associated with the decay of living materials, of protein material," says Block. "When food decays, it's usually because there are bacteria present, and those bacteria can use toxins. Generally, higher animals can detect when food is bad and avoid it. And they detect it with their noses." Maybe this sensitivity to rancid food was favored by evolution. "Animals with the best sense of smell toward molecules associated with decay survive better than those that have an impaired sense of smell," says Block. It's not only the ability to pick up the scent—if Block's theory is correct, the organisms that found the smell unpleasant would survive better.

Wood has a similar theory, although his is based on the relationship of thiols to hydrogen sulfide—a compound we are also sensitive to in low doses. Hydrogen sulfide is often found in places that have no oxygen. "Animals that breathe oxygen want to stay away from areas that don't have oxygen," Wood says. "So our receptors for finding hydrogen sulfide are very highly tuned." Skunks might have evolved to take advantage of this sensitivity by producing a spray with a chemical that has a similar base structure, says Wood. Both theories suggest that skunks capitalize on our evolved sensitivity to odors that signify something harmful. This is the genius of skunk spray: it's not particularly harmful; it reminds us of something that is. This is very annoying.

There's usually a reason that things are annoying, even if the reason isn't immediately obvious. Consider the events that occurred in the lab of Nikolaas Tinbergen, a Dutch scientist who studied sticklebacks, a small common fish. In 1973, he and Konrad Lorenz and Karl Von Frisch won the Nobel Prize for their work on animal behavior. The story goes like this: Tinbergen kept sticklebacks in tanks in his lab. Every day, around eleven in the morning, the sticklebacks acted very agitated. Under normal circumstances, the fish would glide placidly through the vegetation in the tanks, but at eleven they darted around the tank as if something was bothering them. After pondering this strange behavior for a time, Tinbergen realized that the timing of the fish agitation coincided with the daily arrival of the mail truck. The fish that exhibited the strange behavior were in a tank by the window in sight of the truck's arrival, and the truck was bright red.

A stickleback with a reddish tinge is a stickleback spoiling for a fight. Evidently, this red truck was enough to get the sticklebacks in the tank annoyed and ready for a fight. "We've tried to eliminate the color red from most things in the stickleback room so that we don't redo the mail truck experiment," says David Kingsley, a geneticist at Stanford University. There's nothing dangerous to a fish about a mail truck, but the general stimulus brings a very specific response, and that's really interesting.

Kingsley is trying track down the genetic changes that gave us our big brains, our ability to walk upright, and our largely hairless bodies. To understand human evolution, Kingsley has turned to fish. Here is Kingsley's thinking. New environments allow new forms to appear. That's part of what Charles Darwin concluded when he studied the beaks of finches on the Galapagos Islands off the coast of Ecuador. Each island has a slightly different ecology, and on each island, the finch beak was uniquely adapted to the ecology of that island. So Kingsley wanted to find a species that had recently—recently, in evolutionary terms—been forced to adapt to new environments. It turned out that the stickleback was ideal.

Sticklebacks are about two or three inches long. They normally live in the ocean but migrate to coastal areas to breed each spring. Fifteen thousand years ago, ocean sticklebacks all looked pretty much the same. Then came the end of the ice age, and glaciers started to recede. That created a number of new streams, lakes, and coastal estuaries, all potential new homes for sticklebacks. Each of these new environments presented challenges. Different colored water and vegetation required different coloration to make it possible for the sticklebacks to avoid detection by predators. The various predators prompted the stickleback to evolve different kinds of body defenses, such as changes in skeletal armor that make the sticklebacks harder to catch. In some places, merely being a larger size was adequate to allow the sticklebacks to thrive.

Kingsley wanted to find the genes that were responsible for all of these changes, because he hoped that they would allow him to track down the kinds of genes that also changed when humans made a similar migration from one fairly homogenous environment to a variety of new environments with new challenges. That migration took place about a hundred thousand years ago, when our ancestors left Africa. As we moved away from the intense sun near the equator, we lost some of our melanin, which had protected our skin from all of that sunlight. Colder climates also resulted in thicker hair and stockier builds. Even our diets changed, requiring new sets of enzymes to help us digest our food.

Kingsley has collected sticklebacks from all over the world, in a variety of shapes and colors. Just as Gregor Mendel crossed pea plants to find genes, Kingsley crossbreeds sticklebacks and tracks the genes he's interested in through successive generations. He breeds the fish in dozens of thirty-gallon tanks in the basement of the Stanford Medical School.

Nikolaas Tinbergen's mail truck story sounds like one of those apocryphal tales that's simply too good to be true. According to Alun Anderson, however, it is true.

Anderson is a science journalist and author, but before he began his journalism career, he earned a Ph.D. in ethology, the study of animal behavior. "I worked in the same laboratory at Oxford as Niko from 1972 to 1976," says Anderson. "Niko told me that growing up in the Hague, he had loved to bring home sticklebacks from local streams in a jam jar and watch them."

Around 1934, when Tinbergen was working in the Department of Zoology at Leiden University in Holland, he and a student, Joost ter Pelkwijk, started to wonder about the red color on the three-spined stickleback.

"In springtime, male sticklebacks develop 'nuptial colors' of a bright-red belly and throat and defend their territories," says Anderson. "The male builds a nest inside its territory and will court and guide females, which have a silvery color, toward it. If she enters and lays her eggs, he will follow her and fertilize them. Then he will protect the eggs from marauders (often other sticklebacks) and guard the young." The sticklebacks would attack any other males that venture into their territory. "Niko had set up aquarium tanks containing sticklebacks alongside the windows in his laboratory at Leiden University," Anderson says. "In one of them was a single male in nuptial colours. Pelk and Niko both noticed that this male would regularly start a frantic head-down display, holding itself in the peculiar vertical position designed to tell intruders to get out of his territory, even though there was no other male nearby. The attack was aimed toward the window, and it wasn't long before they figured out that it began whenever the bright-red post van drove past the window on the way to deliver the letters."

This led Pelkwijk and Tinbergen to do a famous set of experiments showing that you could provoke a stickleback to attack simply by showing it a red object. "These initial experiments by Tinbergen and others led to a whole body of theory on 'sign stimuli' and 'innate releasing mechanisms,'" says Anderson. More recent work suggests that red alone won't annoy every male, but once one gets annoyed, others may join in the agitation. Perhaps it's not all that surprising that red agitates a male stickleback. Certainly, red is a color that elicits a kind of annoyance that matadors in Spanish bull rings are professionally familiar with.

Skunk spray that reminds us of rotting food, red mail trucks that remind fish of fighting, fingernails on a chalkboard that remind us of a scream—these annoyances may have something in common. The unpleasantness is linked to aversive responses that have evolved to keep us alive.

The annoyances remind us of something we're programmed to avoid, triggering a strong reaction. They are a case of mistaken identity—we can't distinguish between the threat and the thing that mimics the threat.

Rachel Herz doesn't buy the evolutionary theory about skunks. In fact, she thinks we're born without any smell preferences at all. Herz nicely details her argument in *The Scent of Desire*, but the crux of it is that all of a person's smell likes and dislikes are learned—including an aversion to skunk spray. "I know it's a startling statement to make," she says.

Take the smell of rotten eggs—it's hard to imagine not having a gag reflex to that smell, but Herz says that babies show no aversion to the odor. Young children show no preference for the smell of bananas over the smell of poop. Nursing babies have been shown to actually prefer garlic-scented milk. As for skunks, Herz herself likes the smell. She says that her skunk spray predilection comes from an experience she had as a child: she was out on a sunny summer day with her mother, who exclaimed, "Isn't that smell nice?" when the skunk spray smell wafted through the air. Herz has liked the odor ever since. Eric Block, who specializes in sulfur compounds, has a similarly warm feeling about skunk spray: "I don't mind it that much because when I smell it, it kind of reminds me of the work that I do."

In small doses, some thiols are widely pleasing, even to nonchemists. "You can have pleasant-tasting thiols," says Block. For example, a freshly opened container of coffee smells wonderful, thanks to a particular thiol. "Thiols at very low concentrations, including methanethiol, are actually very important in the taste of wine and the odor of different types of wine. At high concentrations, the perception is skunky or stinky or garbagey or something like that." For smells, too, it seems that intensity matters.

Detection also matters, says Herz. Not all humans are thought to have the same odor receptors, meaning that not everyone will smell the same scents. This variation in receptors can make people sensitive to certain scents. For example, if the smell of skunks is particularly annoying to you, it may be because you have more receptors that are sensitive to thiols. What might smell moderately strong to one person could make you gag if you have more receptors for that odor. "It has to do with the intensity," Herz says. "Even your favorite piece of music is aversive if it's blaring." Herz says that this is an instance where there are innate differences in response to smell.

Herz argues that judgments about particular smells come less from an inherent like or dislike but more from the context. She has investigated how association affects our perception of a scent. In one particularly memorable study published in the journal *Perception*, Herz and Julia von Clef asked eighty undergraduates to do a smell test on some "ambiguous" scents and rate their pleasantness.[4] The scents were labeled differently in various sessions. For example, violet leaf was labeled "fresh cucumber" in one session and "mildew" in another; pine oil was "Christmas tree" in one and "spray disinfectant" in another. The real kicker was a 1:1 chemical composition of isovaleric and butyric acids that was labeled "parmesan cheese" in one experiment and "vomit" in another.

The researchers found that the labels made a big difference between annoying and appetizing. People strongly liked the smell of what they thought was parmesan but were repelled by the same odor when they were told it was vomit. This fits in with Herz's theory that our preference for smells is largely dependent on learning and context. On the matter of skunk spray, Herz argues that certain animals, those specifically adapted to a particular habitat, do seem to be born with innate olfactory responses. She argues that humans, as generalists, are different. We're better off being able to learn quickly whether a smell is bad or good, rather than being preprogrammed to avoid a smell.

Herz suggests that our collective dislike of skunk spray may also be related to the fact that it's irritating physically. Smells can have feelings associated with them. Menthol feels cool. Ammonia burns. Skunk spray hurts. The feelings associated with smells are picked up by nerve cells in our noses and eyes—these receptors are responsible for the tears we cry over raw onions. Herz suggests that for compounds such as ammonia and thiols in skunk spray, we don't separate the smell from the sensation. "In actuality, what we're being repelled by or annoyed by is the irritancy, but we say we don't like the 'odor.'"

Skunk spray becomes more threatening in very high doses. There have been reports of dogs dying as a result of being sprayed, according to Wood and Dragoo, although this appears to have more to do with the consistency of the spray than its scent—the oil is thought to coat their lungs. Humans have suffered, too. In 1881, Dr. W. B. Conway, at the Virginia Agricultural and Mechanical College in Blacksburg, recounted a story in the *Virginia Medical Monthly* about the unfortunate victim of a practical joke. A few college boys "secured a two-ounce bottle of the perfume from the skunk," Conway wrote. The boys entered the victim's room, held him down, and forced him to sniff the spray straight from the bottle. "I could not ascertain what amount was administered," Conway wrote. "However, when I reached him I found the following symptoms: A total unconsciousness, relaxation of the muscular system, extremities cool, pupils natural, breathing normal, pulse 65, temperature 94; in which condition he remained for one hour." To treat the comalike symptoms, the doctor "administered small quantities of whisky at short intervals *per orem*, with some difficulty getting him to swallow." It took about an hour and who knows how many whiskeys, but the boy was eventually revived. The take-home point: like many annoyances, skunk spray is usually irritating but can become sickening in high doses.

Whether we are repelled by skunk spray because of its irritancy, because of a cultural construct, or because of an evolutionary predisposition, the annoying quotient doesn't change much. It's annoying no matter *why* it's annoying, and part of that is our sensitivity to these chemicals. Our noses can detect skunk spray at relatively low levels—about ten molecules per billion.

It's not quite clear why we're able to detect thiols in such low doses. One theory has to do with how the thiols bond with the receptors in our noses. Block says, "There's no reason why a very low level of a sulfur compound should fit particularly better in an enzyme cavity if you use the old-fashioned lock and key model for enzymes and substrates. There's no simple explanation for the detection of thiols at extraordinarily low levels, unless you invoke some sort of process where chemically the binding should be extremely good." One idea is that metals aid in the olfactory binding: "metals, such as copper, do bind with sulfur very, very well," says Block. "Is it simply a coincidence that a particularly foul-smelling component in skunk spray, 2-quinolinethiol, is also known to strongly bind to metals?" Block asks. Metals in our olfactory receptors could act like glue, helping the molecules attach more securely to the receptors.

There is no question that once those molecules are lodged in a receptor, they're hard to get out. This leads to olfactory fatigue. The receptors in your nose tire of sending signals. The neurons stop firing, and the brain takes that to mean the odor is gone. This is why tomato juice is thought to work as a skunk spray remedy, says chemist Paul Krebaum. "There's nothing in tomato juice that takes the smell away. It's a total myth. What happens to most people—by the time they're done washing their pets in tomato juice—is that they've been exposed to the skunk spray for so long that they've developed olfactory fatigue." Meanwhile, the tomato juice locks into other receptors, causing them to fire. The skunk smell is masked by the tomato smell.

Although tomato juice won't do the trick, there is something that will. "I was working on a project where we were etching grains of zinc sulfide with acid, and it was producing hydrogen sulfide gas as the by-product," says Paul Krebaum. It stank. People started to complain. "I needed a way of absorbing this hydrogen waste product as it was being generated." The solution was a chemical reaction: alkaline hydrogen peroxide transformed those stinky molecules into something else. After his colleague's cat had a run-in with a skunk, Krebaum wondered whether his remedy might work on the skunk spray, too, because the thiol molecules are shaped like those of hydrogen sulfide. "So I made up a milder version for him," Krebaum says, and it worked. Recognizing the utility of the discovery, Krebaum wrote to *Chemical and Engineering News* and the remedy was published in an article titled "Lab Method Deodorizes a Skunk-Afflicted Pet."[5] The story got picked up by the *Chicago Tribune*, and the rest is history. Now the recipe is available on Krebaum's Web site.[6]

Here's how it works: Mix 3 percent hydrogen peroxide with soap and baking soda, apply it to your skunked pet, and rinse. It works by a process called oxidation. The hydrogen peroxide reacts with the thiol to produce a disulfide, which is much less smelly. If the reaction continues, the disulfide turns into sulfonic acid with the addition of more oxygen to the sulfur group of the thiol. Block also uses oxidizing agents for odor elimination in his lab.* "We use this in the laboratory because we work with a lot of thiols, and you can't even flush things down the drain without causing mischief elsewhere in the building because the drains have vents and so forth. You could use peroxide, but bleach is much more effective. Now bleach is not a good remedy for a pet, nor would you want to use concentrated hydrogen peroxide. But a 3 percent concentration is safe." (Despite the peroxide, Krebaum hasn't gotten many complaints of fur bleaching.)

Krebaum's recipe also includes soap, to get the greasy spray off the pet, and baking soda, which he says neutralizes the

---

*Just like William Wood, Eric Block's research in garlic chemistry had colleagues downwind from his fume hood flaring their nostrils. "I was contacted by our president's office about a strong pizza smell in his office. The solution was to invest several million dollars in new fume stacks to transport the fume hood exhaust gases higher up in the atmosphere away from campus offices!"

sulfonic acid and helps convert another stinky component in the spray into something more benign. Thioacetates are thiols with acetic acid attached. "The stinkiest sulfur compounds always have a free hydrogen on the sulfur and some number of carbons on the other side. If you remove that hydrogen and attach acetic acid to it, it's kind of a temporary attachment because it will break down with water to form a thiol," Krebaum says. That's why if a dog gets wet, it will start to stink of skunk again, months after the initial spraying—the thioacetates hydrolyze into thiols, and the smell returns. These chemicals "act to give the skunk spray long-lasting coverage," says Krebaum. The baking soda raises the pH, which helps speed up the breakdown of thioacetate into acetate and thiols, which can then be oxidized.

This is a rare success story, in which the offending annoyance can be effectively treated. The $3 elixir neutralizes the annoyance on contact, turning it into something benign.

5

Bugged by Bugs: An Epic Bugging

One of our colleagues, NPR science correspondent Christopher Joyce, told us about what annoys him, and he thinks he has it worse than anyone. It's not that his pet peeve is more unpredictable, longer lasting, or more unpleasant than other people's. It's just that he's annoyed at a time when he should have some respite from being annoyed. He's annoyed while he sleeps.

> You can be annoyed all day long, but you can go to bed at night knowing that except for a noisy neighbor or his dog or a mosquito in the air or a lumpy

bed, you've escaped the daily mine field of annoyance. Not me.

No, when I go to bed, I enter the annoyed man's nightmare—the recurring dream. The details change, but the theme is always the same. I'm trying to get somewhere important. I'm trying to catch a plane, and time is running out. Trying to get to a meeting or a class on time. Trying to find a bathroom, urgently, of course. Worst of all, trying to rendezvous with a beautiful woman. Oh, yes, that's when it's most annoying.

Because what happens, every time, is that something keeps me from getting there. I'm driving, and I get lost. My cabdriver stops to get lunch and disappears. There's an accident on the freeway. The public toilets are under repair and out of service. Once there was an earthquake, and I had to get out of a car and walk (I think that was a woman-rendezvous dream).

At first, I struggle diligently to find an alternate route—after all, I'm a responsible person, at least in my dreams. I hail down another cab, book another flight. But soon enough it dawns on me that whatever I do is hopeless. I am foiled, again and again. Sorry, flight canceled due to bad weather. Road work ahead. Bridge down. Detour.

Now, I've traveled a lot in my life, all over the place, in war zones and Amazonian rainforests and Tibetan highlands and on rickshaws and in dugout canoes. I *know* about washed-out bridges and drunken bus drivers and chain-smoking customs agents who'll wait days until you come up with the bribe. My subconscious is *loaded* with examples with which to impale a traveler like a butterfly pinned to a patch of felt.

Eventually, I reach a stage of weary acceptance. I'm not going to make it to my destination. I realize I'm in that dream again, I'm asleep, and that bastard who lives somewhere in my head is doing this on purpose, writing the script as I sleep, making sure that whatever clever solution I come up with, he'll trump it. And there's nothing I can do because that bastard is me . . . the annoying me, annoying me.

Gotta go now . . . got a plane to catch.

What is happening here? Chris has a goal and can't achieve it. He's trying to get somewhere. We've been talking about things that are physically unpleasant, but this is a whole new subclass of unpleasantness: something standing in your way. Think of why traffic jams are annoying. They're unexpected, and all of the inching forward gives you hope that it will clear up around the next bend. The key aspect of the jam, however—which affects how you react to it—is not its intensity but instead how urgently you need to be somewhere else. Annoyances don't often block you completely; most of the time they simply make the journey toward your goal worse. "A lot of annoyance comes when you are trying to do something or make something," says Randolph Nesse, a professor of psychiatry and psychology at the University of Michigan. "You're trying to bake a cake, and all of a sudden you realize you don't have any eggs. It's so annoying! Because now you're going to have to go out and get them. It's interfering with your doing something that you want to do. Something that is not squarely between you and your goal but is kind of distracting you from doing what you want to do or accomplishing what you want to do. I think that probably is what annoyance is."

Whether it's a fly diverting your attention, a dripping faucet preventing you from sleeping, a traffic jam keeping you from reaching your destination, an instruction booklet where the words and the diagrams don't match, or those twist ties that are attached to every part of a toy in its box for protection during shipping, which drags your speed in assembling toys on a birthday or Christmas morning down to a crawl, annoyances slow you down in some way. "It's not like a big rock in the path," says Nesse. "It's more like a lot of rain along the way. It's just an annoying interference that makes it harder for you to make progress toward your goal."

The double annoyance for Joyce, as he points out, is that he's supposed to be sleeping, a time when you have the opportunity to do your best fantasy work. In a dream, Joyce could fly the plane, get the girl, and go to the bathroom, all with no trouble at all—yet his subconscious decides to thwart him, even in his sleep.

Being a flight attendant is annoying. One part of the job seems almost specifically designed for frustration, because the attendants have to serve a lot of passengers in a short space of time. "So I'm taking orders and pouring drinks at a pretty good clip," says Sarah, an experienced flight attendant with a major North American airline. "But every so often, I get someone who asks for coffee. I ask, 'Do you want cream and sugar with that?' And the passenger can't decide. So I stand there, waiting, while this jerk tries to remember whether he likes cream and sugar in his coffee. I mean, he's had coffee probably ten thousand times in his life. How can it be hard to decide whether you want cream and sugar?" Just the memory of this experience gets her a bit agitated.

Annoyances are part of life. They are unavoidable and ubiquitous. Most of the time, despite our best efforts, annoyances get under our skin, cloud our judgment, and distract us from the task at hand.

Yet there are professions where succumbing to annoyance can have extremely dire consequences. You don't want the pilot of your airplane to be swatting at a fly in the cockpit while trying to land the plane in a thunderstorm. You don't want your neurosurgeon to become infuriated by a high-pitched whine coming from the fluorescent lights in the operating theater. You probably don't want an annoying waiter to pester your chef while he's adding cayenne pepper to the sauce for your meal.

There seem to be two extremes in coping with annoyance. One is to fight back with every inch of your being, or, as Hamlet put it, "To take arms against a sea of troubles, and by opposing end them." *Coping* may not be precisely the right word when you rip the headphones off the annoying jerk who is playing his music too loudly in the seat next to you. *Catharsis* may be a better word. Yet it *is* coping, in the sense that after you've done it, you no longer feel annoyed.

The other extreme is rising above the annoyance—not letting it get to you in the slightest. Even when the consequences are not that great, certain professions require people to try to do this. We may be able to learn from this skill. The same techniques that professionals use to shut out the annoyances of life may be of use to the rest of us in doing the same.

If you're a baseball fan, you know exactly what we mean when we say that Joba Chamberlain has lived Chris Joyce's nightmare, the sports equivalent of missing his rendezvous with a beautiful girl.

It was an unseasonably warm night for October in Cleveland, 81 degrees when the game began. That's not a corny, color lead; that unseasonable warmth is an important detail. A breeze was blowing from Lake Erie toward home plate at Jacobs Field for game two of the 2007 American League Divisional Series between the New York Yankees and the Cleveland Indians. The Indians had demolished the Yankees the night before in game one, scoring twelve runs on fourteen hits.

Game two was a different story. Yankee veteran pitcher Andy Pettitte gave up six hits in the first six innings but somehow never allowed the Indians to put a rally together. Cleveland pitcher Fausto Carmona was sharper, allowing just two hits through six, but one of those hits was a solo home run by Yankee center fielder Melky Cabrera.

Pettitte started the seventh inning with a one-run lead. The first batter, Ryan Garko, fouled out to first base. Then Cleveland shortstop Jhonny Peralta doubled, followed by a walk to left-fielder Kenny Lofton, putting the potential go-ahead run on base. Yankees manager Joe Torre had seen enough. He signaled to the bullpen for young phenom pitcher Joba Chamberlain.

Chamberlain was just twenty-two years old. He had appeared in only nineteen major league games, but the hard-throwing rookie was on an incredible roll. In the twenty-four innings he had pitched for the Yankees during the regular season, he had struck out thirty-four of the seventy-eight batters he'd faced and had allowed only one earned run. He had electric stuff, was unhittable really, and many saw in him a future superstar. So Torre decided to roll the dice and see whether his budding superstar was up to preserving the Yankees' lead.

At first, Torre's confidence in Chamberlain seemed justified. He struck out Indians pinch-hitter Franklin Gutierrez on three pitches. It took only two pitches to induce the next batter to pop out to right field. The score remained 1–0 after seven innings. When Chamberlain returned to the mound at the start of the eighth inning, however, he had to face an annoyance of epic proportions. A swarm of insects descended on Jacobs Field.

According to the Associated Press, the insects were gnat-like creatures known as midges. They might have been the nonbiting midge known as *Chironomus plumosus* or possibly its close, nonbiting cousin *Chironomus attenuatus*. The AP writer wasn't clear on this point. "'Non-biting midges are small (1/8-inch to 1/2-inch long), delicate, mosquito-like, but lack scales on their wings,' declares the Ohio State University Extension Fact Sheet on midges and crane flies. It continues, 'Adults are humpbacked, brown, black, orange, or gray, lack a long beak (proboscis), and males have very feathery antennae.'"

Even if a magnifying glass had been handy, Chamberlain would not have been likely to appreciate the midges' feathery antennae and scale-free wings at that particular moment. All he was conscious of was that these bugs were everywhere. What the midges lack in their ability to annoy people with an itchy bite, they make up for in sheer numbers. "Probably millions of them," says David Denlinger, an entomologist at Ohio State University. October is late in the year to see swarms of midges, but the proximity of Lake Erie to the stadium and the warm temperatures at game time probably explain the unseasonable swarm.

"Those are basically mating swarms," says Denlinger. "The major composition of that swarm is probably going to be males looking for mates. And then the females will enter the swarm and get mated, and they don't hang around very long."

No doubt, the ball players wished that the males had the good sense to leave, too, once the party was over—but they didn't. "During my at bat, I had them in my nose," said Yankees first baseman Doug Mientkiewicz. Even viewers at home found it hard to watch on TV, because the midges seemed to be covering every part of every player in every shot. It seemed like some kind of biblical plague.

Baseball is famously a game of inches, and with a tiny white ball whistling past hitters at up to a hundred miles an hour, it's also a game of milliseconds. In fact, the official MLB rules about what a pitcher can wear on the mound are very exacting, so that the flash of a sleeve can't unfairly distract the batter. The space in centerfield behind the pitcher—referred to as the batter's eye—is always black, and fans aren't allowed in that part of the park, so that movement and color hundreds of feet away from the batter can't interfere with his ability to see the pitch. Now Mother Nature had filled the batter's eyeball with crawling, horny insects.

No one was happy with the situation. The Yankees infielders were waving their caps and gloves, trying to shoo away the flying midges. The Cleveland batters looked equally uncomfortable. And the midges were probably wishing that big galoots like Chamberlain would get out of their way so they could continue their hot pursuit of love.

Chamberlain seemed particularly irritated and uncomfortable. "Joba had them all over his back and all over his neck and all over everywhere," said his teammate Mientkiewicz. The umpires weren't about to come to his rescue. "It was just a little irritation," said umpire crew chief Bruce Froemming. "We've had bugs before. I've seen bugs and mosquitoes since I started umpiring." To Froemming, it might have been a little irritation. Unfortunately for Chamberlain, the midges got under his skin, so to speak. He walked Grady Sizemore on four pitches. Then he threw a wild pitch to Asdrubal Cabrera. Sizemore to second. Cabrera laid down a sacrifice bunt. Sizemore to third. A glimmer of hope when Travis Hafner lined out, but then another wild pitch, this time to Victor Martinez. Sizemore home. Game tied.

The Indians went on to win in the eleventh inning in what is officially known as the Bug Game. "They bugged me, but you've got to deal with it," said an irritated Chamberlain after the game.

Mark Aoyagi is a sports psychologist at the University of Denver, and he knows that's easier said than done. According to him, it's simply not possible to actively ignore something that's irritating you. You have to take another approach. In Chamberlain's case, Aoyagi says that the young pitcher "can't not focus on the bugs." In other words, if he tries *not* to focus on the bugs, he will just focus on them more. The trick, says Aoyogi, is to focus on something else. In Chamberlain's case,

Aoyagi says, "The batter, the game, the situation, the catcher's mitt, all those relevant variables. It's not that you're trying to block anything out so you won't focus on the bugs; it's that you choose to focus on what's relevant."

In a way, Aoyagi is arguing for putting something that psychologists call inattentional blindness to good use. The idea is that you can miss things that are literally right under your nose if your attention is focused on something else. In a famous article on the topic, Dan Simons of the University of Illinois described inattentional blindness this way:

> Perhaps you have had the following experience: you are searching for an open seat in a crowded movie theater. After scanning for several minutes, you eventually spot one and sit down. The next day, your friends ask why you ignored them at the theater. They were waving at you, and you looked right at them but did not see them.[1]

To demonstrate how powerful this effect is, Simons and his colleague Christopher Chabris made a video of six people passing two basketballs among themselves. You may have seen it—a rare academic study that went viral on the Internet. In the video, three of the people are wearing white shirts; the others are wearing black shirts. The white-shirted players pass only to other white-shirted players, and the black-shirted players do likewise. As they pass the balls among themselves, they dance around one another, so keeping track of who's passing to whom requires attention. It's like trying to keep track of which walnut shell the pea is under, if you're familiar with that game.

In Simons's experiment, he told subjects to watch the video and count how many times the players in white shirts passed the ball to one another. The video starts in a straightforward manner, with the players weaving and passing, weaving and passing. After about twenty seconds, however, a woman in a gorilla suit walks into the frame from the right, pauses, faces the camera, thumps her chest, and walks out of the frame to the left. All the while, the players continue to weave and pass.

At the end of the fifty-second video, Simons asks subjects whether they saw the gorilla. Typically, 50 percent of the people ask, "What gorilla?" Only after showing them the video a second time, this time with no instruction to count the number of passes, do subjects see the gorilla. Then everyone sees it. It's completely obvious. No one can believe that the gorilla was "invisible" the first time around. Why do some people miss it? And what does this have to do with coping with annoyance?

Basically, people don't see the gorilla because "there is no conscious perception without attention," as Simons puts it. "What's more, the level of inattentional blindness depends on the difficulty of the primary task."

Sports psychologist Benjamin Conmy would have applied a version of Simons's concept of inattentional blindness to Chamberlain's circumstances in the Bug Game. Conmy advises players that there should be "a total immersion in only the aspects of the present that are germane to accomplishing the task. So, for Chamberlain, that's executing a baseball pitch. You want athletes to be so immersed in what they are doing that they almost forget where they are. They're so dialed in that they don't think about anything else." When the insects appeared on the field, however, they interfered with

Chamberlain's consciousness. "Now he's aware of where he is, how he is doing, how these insects might be affecting his preparation," says Conmy. To get Chamberlain back on track, "I would have had him walk away from the situation and get centered again. Because there was nothing he could do about the situation. The bug spray wasn't working. The umpires clearly weren't going to give him a respite. I would have had him say to himself, The next three or four pitches may not be perfect, but they don't have to be disastrous."

The point is that as irritating as the bugs were, they didn't suddenly make Chamberlain an inept pitcher. He was still a fantastic player. "And that's what he needed to focus on," says Conmy. "He needed to realize that he was still completely in control of how well he was pitching this year. The insects were something he couldn't control, and he should have just dealt with that and functioned to the best of his ability."

It sounds easy, but try that the next time you miss your connecting flight. The fact that it's something you can't control is exactly why it drives you crazy. Yet it's also true that if it's all in your head, only you can do something about it.

Another approach that Conmy would have used in the circumstances is something he calls cognitive restructuring. "I would have said to him, 'Remember, Joba, one of the hardest things to do in the world is to hit a baseball. These flies are clearly in this batter's vision. They're flying in and out of his eyes. He has no chance of hitting any of the pitches you can throw right now.'"

A final note on the Bug Game saga. It is not possible to speak for all entomologists, but it's certain that many of them become annoyed when people confuse bugs and insects. The nonbiting midge *Chironomus plumosus* is not a bug. "All bugs are insects, but not all insects are bugs," the Entomological Society of America Web site informs us.[2] "True bugs are part of the order *Heteroptera*, which includes stink bugs, water striders, and bed bugs." (Bed bugs, by the way, are practically the mascot for Team Annoying. They're disgusting, they're random in whom they afflict, and you can never be quite sure you've seen the last of them.) The nonbiting midge is part of the order *Diptera*, insects that include gnats, mosca, mosquitoes, and true flies.

Entomologist David Denlinger says that when he was a kid, it did annoy him when people used the term *bug* inappropriately. Now that he's older, he accepts the fact that nonexperts use the words *bug* and *insect* interchangeably. "I'm cool with that."

Unless the midge attack was orchestrated by the Cleveland Indians or their supporters, Joba Chamberlain's woes can be considered an act of God, as they say in insurance policies, or an act of Nature, as Darwin put it in *On the Origin of Species*.[3] Just because something's out of your control, though, doesn't mean it's outside of everyone's control.

In sports and in life, there are times when the provocation is intentional, executed with the specific goal of putting you off your game. It's the art of "trash talk." Conmy says it's one of the most common ways that athletes try to create a small advantage over their opponents at a level where any advantage could mean the difference between a win and a loss. Trash talk spans a wide spectrum, according to Conmy, but all flavors of trash talk have a common purpose: to distract and annoy.

At one end of the spectrum are players who simply try to divert the attention of their opponents. "Some of them, their entire aim is to just be very funny, very gregarious, very entertaining, and get the player opposite them to stop thinking about the skills that allow them to perform well in the game," says Conmy. In the middle of the spectrum are people who don't say anything intrinsically annoying, but whose constant prattle becomes annoying during the course of a match. Conmy knew a soccer player who continually discussed cheese with the player he was guarding, from the first minute on. "He'd say, 'Do you like cheese? I like cheese. What kind of cheese do you like? I like cheddar.' And on and on and on. Imagine that for ninety minutes! And then there are the trash talkers who try to insult the other player," he says. "To take his natural aggressiveness and push him over the edge."

Into that last category falls Marco Materazzi. His trash talking elicited a shocking explosion from one of the best soccer players in the world, an explosion witnessed live by television viewers around the world.

The scene was the finals of the 2006 World Cup: Italy versus France. Materazzi was a star for the Italians. His victim was Zinedine Zidane. Both France and Algeria claimed Zidane as a citizen, but the tall midfielder chose to play for the French national team. He's one of only four players ever to score in two World Cup finals. Tough, tall, and creative, he was one of soccer's superstars. In 1998, he led the French to victory over Brazil. In 2002, however, injuries prevented him from making much impact for his national team. That year, France exited the tournament in the first round without managing to score a single goal. In 2004, Zidane decided to retire from international soccer.

In 2006, the French coach coaxed the thirty-four-year-old Zidane into joining the national team one more time. It turned out to be a shrewd move. Zidane displayed the same magic that had carried France to the finals eight years earlier. In a crucial match against Spain, he set up one goal and scored another himself. And in the quarter finals, he set up the winning goal against Brazil. Before the final, he was awarded the Golden Ball, which was given to the best overall player in the competition.

The 2006 final was held on July 9 at the Olympistadion in Berlin. France and Italy were both strong teams. Both had stifling defenses and dazzling strikers. France struck first, when Zidane hammered a penalty shot that bounced off the crossbar and into the goal. Twelve minutes later Materazzi evened the score, heading home a corner kick from Andrea Pirlo. After that, both teams had opportunities, but neither could break through. At the end of regulation time, the match was tied 1–1. Zidane nearly won it for the French in overtime with a header that Italian goalie Gianluigi Buffon just managed to tip over the crossbar. Then, a bit later in the overtime period, it happened.

Zidane and Materazzi were jogging upfield together when they appeared to have a verbal exchange. Zidane went a few feet ahead, then turned around and head-butted the Italian player with such force that Materazzi was knocked off his feet and landed on his back.

The referee missed the incident, but a linesman saw it, as did hundreds of millions of television viewers around the world. After being informed of the incident, the referee strode up to Zidane, pulled the red card from his pocket, and held it up to Zidane, indicating that he was expelled from the match and could not be replaced. The Italians weren't able to capitalize on their one-man advantage, however. The match ended at 1–1, but the Italians prevailed in a penalty shoot-out.

What did Materazzi say? How long had he been pestering Zidane during the match? And why did a veteran player like Zidane succumb to the provocation? "We don't know what was going on throughout the course of that game," says Conmy. "Who really knows how much Materazzi said to him. That's ninety minutes, that's almost the whole game. Materazzi could have been in his ear from minute one, being abusive and offensive. Eventually, it just became too much."

According to press reports, Materazzi chose an Italian TV listings magazine, *Sorrisi e Canzoni* ("Smiles and Songs") to give his side of what happened.

Materazzi admitted that he had grabbed Zidane's shirt as they were both trying to get to the ball. According to Materazzi, the Frenchman told him, "If you want my shirt that badly, I'll give it to you at the end of the match," to which Materazzi replied, "I'd prefer your whore of a sister."[4]

Zidane told a different story. In an interview with the newspaper *El Pais*, Zidane said that Materazzi made a slur against his mother. "Things happen on the pitch. It's happened to me many times, but I could not stand it there," Zidane is quoted as saying. "It is not an excuse, but my mother was ill. She was in [the] hospital. This, people did not know, but it was a bad time."[5]

Regardless of the precise nature of the trash talk, it clearly worked spectacularly well. Conmy says that world-caliber athletes need to have a quick trigger, to be able to perform at an exceptional level. This may put them at a higher risk for getting annoyed. "They very much walk a thin line," says

Conmy. "The problem with that thin line is if something just pushes you over, just presses your button a little bit too much, that's where we see these levels of violence or anger."

Conmy knows that sometimes athletes feel as if they just have to respond to the abuse. "If they're going to do it, once they've done it, I'd like them to get centered as quickly as possible on what they're doing, which is playing the game, whatever game that may be." Getting centered will also help you deal with the annoying driver behind you or the annoying music in the supermarket.

Unfortunately for Zidane, after the outburst there was no more game to center on. Yet on some level, he must have felt good to have shut Materazzi up. That's because there's a little more to this than simply having something get between you and your goal. The whole point of a sport is that you have another team full of people who are actively working to keep you from your goals, and that's not annoying. They're supposed to be doing that. You expect them to be doing that, but you don't expect a plague of midges to join them.

A lineup of pesky Cleveland hitters could have been predicted. It's only when you find your world—and your expectation of how you might move through it—suddenly out of sync with your reasonable assumptions that things become annoying.

6

Who Moved Their Cheese?

On any given day, there are some eight hundred thousand mice living on campus at the Jackson Laboratory in Bar Harbor, Maine.

You wouldn't know it to look at the place. As you drive up to the bucolic campus on Route 3, less than a mile from downtown Bar Harbor, it's not as if you see tiny white critters darting among the trees. If you sniff carefully and are familiar with the smell, you can get a faint odor of a laboratory animal-care facility, but that's it. The cluster of buildings and lawns could pass for a small college campus or maybe a midsize independent research institute (which it is) but not a place that harbors hundreds of thousands of rodents. Nonetheless, if you want to know just about anything about a mouse, from how its immune system works to how its genes control the number of teeth it has to what really ticks it off, the Jackson Lab is a good place to come.

The lab was founded in 1929 by a scientist named Clarence Cook Little, better known as C. C. Little. He was an interesting character from an old Boston family and a direct descendant of Paul Revere.

While he was a graduate student at Harvard, Little wrote a paper proposing that genetics was a crucial factor in whether a transplanted organ would be rejected. The paper was published in *Science*.[1] At the time, no one knew that someday there would be organ transplants, but Little's work laid the groundwork for understanding organ rejection.

When Little was in his twenties, he also began to develop strains of genetically inbred mice. Inbred strains are useful, because each mouse from a particular inbred strain is genetically identical to every other mouse from that strain. You can transplant skin or an internal organ between mice of the same strain, and because their immune systems are identical, there will be no rejection. If you test a particular drug or treatment on mice of one inbred strain, any variability that you see as a consequence can't be blamed on genes. Something else has to be the cause. Having this kind of genetically level playing field has been extremely useful for researchers. Some of the strains of mice that Little developed are still being used by researchers today.

In 1922, at the astonishingly young age of thirty-three, Little became president of the University of Maine and three years later got the same gig at the University of Michigan. At

Michigan, Little demonstrated quite an ability to irritate people. He annoyed the university regents and the governor with his outspoken views on birth control (he was for it), euthanasia (he was for it), and eugenics (he was for that, too). His tenure as university president lasted only a few years.

If he got under the skin of his higher-ups, he nevertheless managed to befriend some of nearby Detroit's wealthy industrialists. When Little left Michigan, he even convinced Edsel Ford and Roscoe B. Jackson, the president of the Hudson Motorcar Company, to bankroll the new institute he wanted to build to study mouse genetics.

Today, the lab employs some twelve hundred scientists, technicians, and administrative staff, most of whom are involved in some way or another with probing the mouse genome. The lab scientists don't work with all eight hundred thousand rodent residents. Many of the mice are supplied to researchers at other institutions.

There's a surprising amount of security at the lab, especially for the building where most of the mice are housed. It's not so much that scientists are worried about theft or escape. A bigger worry is that animal rights activists will try to break in and wreak havoc. Lab officials insist that the main reason for the security is to protect the mice from humans who may be carrying diseases that could be harmful to the rodents. Once a year, however, the lab does let humans view the mice, and that's during what's called the Mouse Clinic.

The clinic is part of the two-week summer course on mammalian genetics that the lab has conducted for the last half-century. Senior genetics researchers from around the world agree to teach at the course, partly because the Jackson Lab is a good place to hobnob with colleagues in mammalian genetics, and partly because Bar Harbor can be spectacularly beautiful in the summer. (It can also be rainy and foggy for days on end, causing you to curse the vacation brochure that convinced you to spend your entire two-week holiday there.)

Graduate students and recently minted Ph.D.'s attend the course, and the Mouse Clinic is one of the highlights. In it, the lab brings out examples of its most interesting mouse strains, and scientists at the lab explain their research to the course participants. The clinic takes place in a parking lot next to one of the lab buildings under a large tent, a hundred feet long and forty feet across. There are about two dozen tables under the tent, and on every table are several clear plastic boxes, each a bit larger than a shoe box and containing a different strain of mouse. You can easily see the mice inside the boxes. Some are brown, others are white. One mouse even has a green glow if you shine ultraviolet light on it.

In some boxes there is only one mouse; others hold several. All of these mice at the clinic have one thing in common: "They're not very happy," says Peggy Danneman. Danneman is a senior veterinarian specializing in lab animal medicine. She says there are several reasons for these mice to be pissed off. First of all, mice detest open spaces. Yes, there's a tent, but the tent has no walls, and for a mouse, this is about the same as being plopped down in the middle of the great outdoors.

"Mice want to be close to a wall or sheltered," says Danneman. Even though there's no threat to these mice in their protective plastic cages, historically, a mouse out in the open is a mouse in trouble. That's because just about every larger carnivore wouldn't mind munching on a tasty mouse snack. "You see the same thing with bright lights," says Danneman. "Mice do not like bright lights, and I would postulate it's for the same reason." Bright lights would make them easier to spot. Although there's no direct sunlight inside the tent, it's plenty bright. While these things may be temporary and unpredictable, for a mouse, they could cross from unpleasant into genuinely dangerous (as far as they can tell). Yet that's just the beginning of the assault on mouse sensibilities that the Mouse Clinic represents.

Mice hate being put in a freshly cleaned box, and these boxes are spotless. "Humans change the cage because it starts to smell, and they don't like it," says Eva Eicher, one of the lab's star geneticists. "But the mouse would probably prefer to have the cage a little dirtier and changed a lot less often."

Eicher says there are other reasons that mice don't like to have their boxes changed. "Pretend I'm a mouse, living in my house," she says. "I've just gotten the house set up. I've got my bedroom and my bed all made. I've got my bathroom all set up." Mice urinate in the same place. They defecate anywhere, so the analogy's not perfect, but you get the idea. In any case, the clean new cage might be aesthetically pleasing to humans, but to mice it means that every few days they have to rebuild their world. How much fun is that?

Then there's how the move to a new abode occurs. "All of a sudden, some giant thing grabs you," says Eicher. "And they grab you by the tail so your butt's up in the air and your head is down." What's more, it tends to happen during the day, and mice are nocturnal. They sleep during the day.

Moving can also mean social disruption. "Maybe I'm with five or six males," says Eicher. "And one of the males is a bully. He has made everybody else kowtow to him. But when we get moved into a new house, the bully has to reestablish himself, so he runs around biting everybody." The rebuilding, the sleep disruption, the social anxiety—none of it is life threatening, it is simply disruptive and not at all how the mouse expected things to go.

In Italian, in response to a question like *Come va?* (How's it going?), you might say, *Tutto a posto*, if things are going well. It means everything's good, but more precisely, the expression means *everything is in place*. In a country like Italy, where drinking a cappuccino after eleven a.m. upsets the apple cart (perhaps you weren't aware that milk interferes with afternoon digestion), it makes sense that the good life would be the ordered life.

This isn't only an Italian thing (or a mouse thing). People generally like it when things are in place. Our natural tendency is to organize—from the cans in our cabinets to the files on our desktops to our careers and families. It's frustrating when things are out of order.

This trait isn't confined only to living things. Materials like to have things in place, too—particularly when it comes to the atoms that compose them. Yet sometimes a material is faced with competing forces that make it difficult to know how to arrange things. Frustration (in physics, too!) is a deep internal conflict with no clear resolution.

Physicist Leon Balents is a frustration expert, although he doesn't know exactly where the term came from. "I'm not sure whether it's that the theoretician is frustrated in not being able to figure out how the system should resolve these competing forces. Or whether the material is frustrated in not knowing how to resolve the competing forces." It seems to work on two levels.

Glass and plastics are often frustrated, but "the classic thing to talk about in the case of frustration is a magnet," says Balents, who works at the University of California, Santa Barbara. A frustrated magnet isn't really what people think of as a magnet at all. Frustrated magnets won't even stick to anything.

Take that sombrero magnet that your friend brought back from Mexico that you've hidden under a menu on the fridge door. The sombrero, technically a "ferromagnet," sticks to the fridge because of its electrons and the way they spin inside the atoms that make up the magnet. In ferromagnets, all of the electron spins want to orient in the same direction, just as the magnet in a compass wants to point north. "In ferromagnets, each spin wants to line up with its neighbor," says Balents. "You can think of it as a force, where each one tries to force the other one to line up." The cumulative alignment of these electron spins gives the magnet its ability to attract things.

In these magnets, figuring out how to put things in place is straightforward—at least, at certain temperatures. "There's always a simple way to minimize the energy of all pairs of spins," Balents says. "Just point them all along the same axis." Every electron spin goes in the same direction as the one next to it. *Tutto a posto.* The sombrero is not frustrated.

Ferromagnets are much less common than antiferromagnets, Balents says. And antiferromagnets want a different arrangement. Their tendency is to order their electron spins in opposite directions. (This is why antiferromagnets don't repel or attract anything—there's not a cumulative force in one direction.) And this is where things can get frustrating.

If the atoms are aligned in a row—think of a battleship pegboard—it's easy to alternate the spins: one up, one down, one up, one down. If the atoms are arranged in a triangle, however, there's not a clear solution. If the spin on top of the triangle goes up, and the spin on the right corner goes down, what does the left side do? "The first spin wants the second one to be anti-parallel to it," Balents says, "but the third spin is in trouble because it can try to be anti-parallel to the first spin, but then it will be parallel to the second one. This is the simplest example of what a physicist calls frustration."

The competing forces make it so that there is no clear resolution. No way to satisfy every need. No right answer. "So it will make a compromise," Balents says. "Usually, there isn't only one compromise that is the best one; there can be many, meaning many different ways to orient these little magnetic spins that are almost equally good in terms of energy. This is maybe not totally unfamiliar; if you try to negotiate something complicated between many parties, it is not obvious how to figure out what the best compromise is. It's that way for a frustrated magnet as well."

Some materials are more frustrated than others. To determine the severity of the case, Balents says that you can see how the material behaves at different temperatures. At higher temperatures, frustrated materials are less decisive: they go from compromise to compromise, never settling on one. If you start to cool a material down and it still cycles through different compromises, it's considered highly frustrated. The lower the temperature is before the material settles down is the measure of the material's frustration.

•   •   •

Some mice are also more frustrated than others. It's easy to tell when a mouse is getting irritated. "You can see it in its ears and body language," says Belinda Harris. She's a mouse wrangler or, more formally, a biomedical technologist in the mutant mouse resource facility. Harris says that when a mouse is content with its environment, you can tell. "They generally put their ears up and look around and point their nose to where they want to be." On the other hand, when irritated, "they put their ears back and they flinch or act like they are not comfortable in whatever situation," she says.

If you've ever wondered whether mice poop when they are annoyed, Danneman and Harris have the same answer: "Yes." The other obvious question to put to a mouse expert is, Do cats annoy mice? Again, the obvious answer is yes. Perhaps more surprising is that rats annoy mice. "People just think of mice as rat wannabes," says Danneman. "But a rat is a threat to a mouse. It's a predator-prey relationship. You will see that mice, if they're housed in an area where they smell rats, they will be agitated."

Michelle Curtain agrees with Eva Eicher about mice not liking to be handled. Curtain is one of the technicians at the mouse facility and a de facto expert in mouse behavior. She's standing behind a table set up near the outside edge of the tent. The mice she's brought with her are from a strain formally known as SOSTdc1, but Curtain says that everyone at the lab refers to them as Sharkey, because of their interesting phenotype.

Phenotype, by the way, is a word you have to get used to if you spend any time with biologists, particularly geneticists. It basically means the way the animal appears. If scientists were simply to say, "That strain of mouse has an unusual appearance," it would not sound half so erudite and educated as when they say, "That mouse has an unusual phenotype." So scientists generally stick with *phenotype*.

Phenotype should not be confused with genotype. Genotype refers to the particular set of DNA letters that make up a mouse's genetic instructions. Often, changing a mouse's genotype by removing or adding DNA letters will change its phenotype—but not always. A mouse with an interesting phenotype often will also have an interesting genotype. Not always, but often enough that by studying mice with interesting phenotypes, scientists learn interesting things about the genetics of a particular trait.

In the case of Sharkey, the interesting phenotype is that these mice have extra teeth.* To show off this dental precociousness, Curtain reaches into the box containing Sharkey mice and picks one up by the tail. She then lowers it so that its forepaws can reach the top of the box. The mouse, sensing a safe haven, grabs onto the lip of the box, and for a brief instant, it becomes a mouse bridge, anchored at one end by its forepaws on the box and at the other by Curtain's blue latex–gloved hand. This position makes it easy for Curtain to grab the mouse by the scruff of the neck with her free hand and turn it over. She performs these maneuvers smoothly, with a practiced air.

Sure enough, with the mouse's mouth open, it's easy to see a few extra small teeth tucked in next to the ones that appear to belong there. The idea in creating Sharkey mice isn't merely to populate a mouse freak show. Scientists have already begun to unravel the steps in tooth formation by using mutant strains such as Sharkey. Wouldn't it be nice if someday

---

*Get it? Sharkey . . . extra teeth. Oh, those wacky scientists.

this research made it possible to grow a new molar, instead of getting a crown on one that you cracked on an olive pit?

Another thing scientists may learn from mice is something about the genetics of annoyance. You see, all mice probably become somewhat annoyed from time to time, but other mice get really annoyed a lot of the time, and the difference is probably genetic. Take the strain known as Fierce. Elizabeth Simpson developed this strain while she was working at the Jackson Laboratory. Now she's at the University of British Columbia. It's not hard to see how this strain got its name. A normal mouse, when lifted up by its tail, will just hang there. Oh, it might twist around a bit, but basically, lifting a mouse by its tail is a pretty safe way to grab one. A Fierce mouse, on the other hand, will swing itself up so that it can grab its own tail and then use the tail as a kind of climbing rope so that it can bite the person who dared to pick it up.

You don't have to pick up these mice to get them riled up. Bump their cages, and they turn into biting terrors. Simpson says the scientists have learned that if they don't want to chase these mice all over the lab, they must put their boxes in large plastic garbage cans before taking off the lids. Because the minute the tops are lifted off, the mice start bouncing around like popcorn, trying to jump onto and bite the person or the people who jostled their home.

You might say that these mice are easily annoyed. Elizabeth Simpson prefers not to say that. She says that calling a mouse "annoyed" is anthropomorphizing—assigning human feelings or emotions to an animal (or an object)—and that anthropomorphizing "is something scientists try not to do. And we tell our students not to do it." Really, she says, there's no way of knowing what annoys a mouse, because we can't ask them.

As long as that's clear, for the sake of argument, she's willing to say that her Fierce mice *appear* to be easily annoyed. She's even found a gene that seems to be responsible for this behavior. It's got a catchy name: NR2E1. This gene seems to play an important role in brain development in mammals, although it's also found in fruit flies (small brains), roundworms (really, really small brains), and sponges (no brains at all). Without reference to the question of whether sponges can get annoyed, Simpson says mice that are missing the NR2E1 gene exhibit the Fierce phenotype. There's that word again. In this case, it refers not only to the mouse's physical appearance but to its behavior as well.

Humans also have a version of NR2E1. In fact, if you put a healthy human NR2E1 gene into a Fierce mouse that's missing NR2E1, the mouse loses its hyperaggressive behavior and turns back into a normal mouse. What happens when the human NR2E1 gene is missing or mutated? Simpson is trying to answer that question. Already she has some hints that the gene might be damaged in patients with bipolar disorder.

Simpson says that the Fierce strain is interesting to study for what it might explain about the genetics of human behavior, but mice of this strain are not easy to study. Not long after Simpson started to breed these mice at the Jackson Laboratory, her lab technician came to her and said, "I quit. I can't stand working with these mice." "I understood what she meant," Simpson says. "These mice are difficult to handle, difficult to breed, and a pain in the neck to work with. Basically, these mice are incredibly annoying."

So while it may not be possible to say for sure whether a mouse is annoyed, at least Simpson knows how to make a mouse annoying.

7

The Terror of Perfect Pitch

Sometimes sounds annoy people and it's not about the sound's intrinsic characteristics and it's not about personal taste. It's about the listener. Certain people have special sensitivities. Remember Linda Bartoshuk and her supertasters? Think of Lucy Fitz Gibbon as a superlistener. As with most superpowers, superlistening sounds like a good thing, unless you're the one who has to live with it.

Fitz Gibbon received her undergraduate degree at Yale University. She has brown hair and wears brown-framed glasses and seems perfectly easygoing, except when she describes the scanner in her office at the Yale Center for

British Art, where she works part time. She calls it her Waterloo. It's loud. It's repetitive. It's often in use. This seems more like a minor annoyance, however, not a disastrous military defeat. Yet when Lucy recalls the tone, which she hums, she can't help but squint and crumple her brow. "It's so bad. The pitch that it makes is just flat of a C natural."

Lucy has perfect pitch and years of musical training—which can be a deadly combination for aural annoyance. Perfect pitch, which researchers call absolute pitch, is classically defined as the ability to identify notes without the use of a reference tone. What it means is that whenever Lucy walks down the street, she hears musical notes in sounds that most people experience as noise. Every buzz, rumble, and honk has a pitch associated with it. "Most objects, if they're moving—like the fan in your computer or the buzzing in your light bulb—make some sort of overtone," says Lucy. And most of the time, those notes are not in tune.

A walk in New Haven quickly reveals how differently Lucy experiences the world. A big blue truck idling on High Street: "It's an E flat." The crosswalk bell by Yale's largest dining hall, "Commons," rings slightly flat of a C natural. "I'm pretty sure that it's the exact same pitch of the bells in my high school that used to ring to tell you to go to class. The first time I heard it, I had this Pavlovian response, and I was back in high school, thinking, 'Must get to biology.'" It's common for people with perfect pitch to have excellent tonal memory as well, researchers say.

With great power comes great annoyance. Lucy says that her case isn't so extreme. "I had a friend who used to say that every morning before he got up, he would have to sit in his room and meditate so that he wouldn't be driven crazy by all of the sounds that he would encounter during the day. I'm not quite like that. If I'm having sort of a nervous or irritable day, I think I tend to pay more attention to sounds that annoy me. But for the most part, you have to block it out. Just like you can't pay attention to every piece of sensory information that's coming through; otherwise, you end up overwhelmed."

But it takes some effort to tune out sounds that are out of tune. Imagine that you are Lucy as a college senior. You sit down to write your senior thesis about the opera *La Callisto* by Venetian composer Francesco Cavalli. You're interested in exploring how "it functions as a criticism of the Venetian practice of forced monachization." (We had to look up the word *monachization*, too: it's a noun meaning "the act or process of becoming a monk or of becoming or making monastic.")

You turn on your laptop, and it starts to hum. "My laptop usually starts off just south of an F sharp," Lucy says, "and then sits around just south of a G sharp for a while, and eventually winds up just south of a C natural. It changes, depending on how fast the fan is running in the computer." It was annoying, but, fortunately, between voice lessons (she's a soprano), a graduate-level chamber music class, her lead as Deidamia in Francesco Sacrati's *La Finta Pazza*, and learning *Pierrot Lunaire*, Lucy mostly hears her own voice—singing in tune.

Tutto a posto—everything is in its place.

About fifteen years ago, David Ross also spent a great deal of time on the Yale campus, singing. Today he's a professor of psychiatry. He hasn't left Yale—after doing his undergraduate work there, he went on to complete an M.D./Ph.D. at the Yale School of Medicine.

As an undergrad, Ross was a singer in Redhot & Blue, an a cappella group at Yale. He recalls that the director of the group had perfect pitch. "At that point, I really didn't even know what that meant. She would ask me to do stuff that didn't make sense. She'd say, 'Can't you just sing a C? Can't you hear that's a quarter of a step flat?'" Ross, however, couldn't do either of those things. "It was incredibly annoying to go through this experience."

It's true. Being told to fix something when you don't know the difference between fixed and broken and being reprimanded for something you can't control are annoying. (In fact, as we'll see later, these are simple and foolproof ways to annoy people if you're conducting an experiment on frustration.)

Ross and the group director were hearing the same notes but experiencing them differently—Ross wanted to know why. He continues to study this question, now in his own lab. He says that the acoustic world is a mental minefield for people with perfect pitch. "They notice stuff that we don't," Ross says. "Radio stations will speed up or slow down a song to make it fit in the time spot that they have. So if they have three minutes, they might play a song that's supposed to be three minutes and five seconds and simply speed it up. Well, that's also increasing the pitch. We don't notice that, but people with perfect pitch do. And it might be really annoying."

Why is it annoying, though? People with absolute pitch talk about pitch differently than we do. Ross says, "They describe pitch as having a fundamental salience that's present for them but absent for us." It's as if pitches have identities. "That a B flat sounds like a B flat because it just does."

Robert Zatorre, a cognitive neuroscientist who studies perfect pitch at the Montreal Neurological Institute, gives this analogy for how people with perfect pitch hear the world: "It's like if I see a cat or a dog. When I was a child, I didn't know what they were called, but I knew a cat was a cat when I saw one and a dog was a dog when I saw one. Someone eventually told me the label for that creature is *cat*." For people with perfect pitch, the difference between an A flat and a C sharp is the difference between a cat and a dog.

Some have used colorblindness to help explain what it's like for those of us without perfect pitch—but Zattore doesn't think this is quite right. If you can see color, a particular hue probably doesn't have a distinct identity. For example, try to match the color of your wall from memory when you're at the paint store. "You try that and see how successful you are when you get back home. It'll be off, there's no question. Why is that? Because we don't have absolute color. If we had absolute color, we'd be able to look at that wall and say, 'Okay, I know the exact shade that is.' And I could go to the paint store and pick that one out of the thousands of possible shades that might exist. There may actually be people who have something like absolute color, and maybe they're artists or interior decorators, I don't know."

For Lucy, each pitch does have a unique identity—and this may explain why an out-of-tune note is so annoying. "They sort of have different characters or textures to them in my head now," she says. "And I associate them in groups of fifths." A fifth would be two notes that are seven semitones apart—that's the number of notes, including sharps and flats, between two notes. Lucy associates A and E, F and C, and D and G. In terms of frequencies lining up, they are the next most perfect interval to an octave. (A fifth is more familiar to your ear as a power chord, the building blocks of rock music for bands that range from the Kinks to the Kings of Leon.) "I hear them sort of in these pairs of fifths with similar textures to them, if you will. This sounds kind of weird—F and C are sort of like flat and ribbonlike. Like a flat, smooth ribbon. And A and E are more like a single strand. But D and G to me sound more rich, softer. Like a fuzzy ribbon."

Lucy doesn't *see* a fuzzy ribbon in her brain, she says, she feels it. "Like if my brain had fingers, it could feel these notes, and that's what they would feel like. It seems like everyone should feel this way, too, because they are all different, they're all their own unique selves. You don't exactly think about it; it's just how they are. It's like they're all individual different people or something like that. And they all have different characteristics."

For her, when a note is out of tune, it doesn't have an identity. "Maybe what makes it annoying, when the pitch is in this nebulous area between two notes, is that it's in no-man's-land." There is something unsettling about an unidentifiable signal. It's irritating to hear something that we can't place.

Out-of-tune sounds bother her because her brain is expecting a tone to sound a certain way. David Ross puts it like this: "A similar phenomenon exists in psychotherapy." (When he's not doing perfect-pitch research, he's a psychiatrist treating patients with post-traumatic stress disorder at the Veterans Administration.) "If you're feeling frustrated at any point in time, it's because there's a gap in expectation. If you're frustrated with a patient, it's because your expectations of what's going to happen don't match with what the patient's expectations are. If you have somebody who is drinking, he keeps drinking and you get really frustrated. It's your problem, not his problem. He doesn't want to stop drinking. Once you adjust your expectations, everything is fine. If your expectation is that the notes will be perfect, you're going to be disappointed."

As someone who is interested in how music has changed over history, Lucy is acutely aware of this. "It's definitely a construct that's occurring within this artificial system that we've created in Western tonal music."

Now that you know all of this about Lucy, you may be shocked by what her particular focus is: early music, which is particularly grating for someone with perfect pitch. You see, compositions from the 1600s, for example, are not tuned to the same standard as modern tuning. An A from that era is not the same frequency as an A today. (This is called having a difference in pitch center.) "Growing up in the modern world, we think of the note A as being at 440 Hz. And a lot of early music does A at 415, which is a half-step lower, or A at 465, which is a half-step higher, in which case I have to transpose."

In addition, early music often has a different "temperament" than today's equal temperament. This is basically how notes are shoehorned into an octave. The relationship between a D and a G might be different, frequency-wise, in one temperament than in another. In early music, one of the tuning systems used is called quarter-comma meantone. "The tuning system itself changes where I expect pitches to be. For me, the most annoying part is that the fifths are lower than in equal temperament, so to me they sound flat." Lucy says that this can make for good tonal symbolism, though. The out-of-tune sound conveys anguish.

For a singer with perfect pitch, that anguish is visceral. "I feel like I have to sing out of tune," says Lucy. "It isn't really out of tune, it's just a different way of thinking about music. I'm sure for people back then who had perfect pitch, that would have been completely normal to them. It does highlight how much of this is artificial—is really just a construct of our brains."

The annoying part is a construct: the product of learning a musical system and then expecting the sounds you hear to fit within it, which suggests an *extrinsic* unpleasantness. On the other hand, if you are musically trained and have perfect pitch, there may be no situation in which an out-of-tune note isn't annoying, which suggests an *intrinsic* unpleasantness— at least, for this population.

Who is at risk for this special annoyance? There's a lot of debate about that—particularly about the role of musical training in developing perfect pitch. Lots of musicians had early musical training, but most don't have perfect pitch. On the other hand, most people who have been identified as having perfect pitch have had early musical training. What David Ross wants to understand is whether you can have perfect pitch with no musical training.

Lucy grew up in a musical house, although she's the only one with perfect pitch. She started on the violin when she was five, but she doesn't remember always hearing the world the way she does now. She began singing in the choir in junior high. "It was really strange. I remember one time I sang a wrong note, and one of the girls sitting next to me was like, 'Lucy makes mistakes!' and I was like, 'Of course, I make

mistakes. Everyone makes mistakes.' But then I started thinking about it and realized that I really did always know what the
pitches were going to be. I don't think I was born with perfect
pitch. And I really didn't notice it until I started singing."

The debate about whether absolute pitch is learned or
something you are born with has raged in the scientific literature for longer than a hundred years, Ross says. He hopes his
research will someday help resolve the debate.

Most perfect-pitch tests go something like this. A
researcher—or, more likely, a graduate student—will play a
series of notes and ask the listener to name them. Sound fair?
No, says Ross. "If you weren't a musician, you wouldn't know
the names of notes, and you couldn't take the test. So you've
tautologically defined that you're only going to look at musicians, and then you're going to claim that musical training is
required."

Ross came up with a different test that, instead of nam-
ing notes, requires participants to match notes by ear using
a "sine function generator" that generates a tone and sweeps
through pitches when you turn the front knob. Ross asks
people to match the first tone in a long series of notes. This
requires people to keep the initial tone in their memories
while the other tones play. "We had twenty-two professional
non-AP musicians [musicians without absolute, or perfect,
pitch], largely faculty from the Yale School of Music."

How do you think they did? Keep in mind that people in
this group could easily play any number of complex classical
works entirely from memory. What's one note? A lot, it would
seem, to someone without perfect pitch.

"Their combined performance, when you added together
all of their data, didn't differ from chance," Ross says, "which

is to say that they would have done just as well if they weren't wearing the headphones when they did our experiments. And these are professional musicians who are really quite invested in their musicianship." Subjects with perfect pitch didn't miss a note. This makes sense: if pitches have an identity, it wouldn't be that hard to learn to the labels and remember them.

Then Ross tested three-, four-, and five-year-olds who were suspected of having perfect pitch but who had little musical training. These kids scored perfectly. "It was hard to explain the instructions because at four years old, it's pretty hard to understand how to do this test. Yet you have a four-year-old outperforming the faculty at the Yale School of Music," Ross says sympathetically. This suggests that there's some predisposition for perfect pitch.

It's almost impossible, however, to disentangle environmental impact from innate ability. Exposure to music could make a difference, even if formal musical training isn't required. "You'd have to raise someone in a soundproof world for this person to have no musical exposure," says Robert Zattore. "I think this is, in a way, one of those false debates. The answer to that question is almost always, 'It's got to be both.' Neither the biological predisposition nor the environmental influence is sufficient; you need both, and that interaction has to come at the right time." Just what genetic and environmental recipe is required for a particular individual is anybody's guess. And just what is different about how the brains of people with perfect pitch process notes? That's the holy grail, Zattore says.

You might think that the annoyance factor of perfect pitch would be worth it if you were a musician, at least a musician who was not interested in weird temperaments and different pitch centers. Yet it's not so clear. "I tend to think about music in a very linear and discrete fashion," Lucy says. Another perfect-pitch possessor describes being at a hockey game. The marching band was playing Britney Spears's "Toxic." He knew the song, but he didn't recognize it. The band had changed the key. This is a common problem for people with perfect pitch.

Lucy provided a literary analogy. "Tolstoy was a writer. And he liked to look at all of these tiny details in something. But when he's writing *War and Peace*, he wants to write this huge work, so he had to work very hard to extend this practice to an entire novel, which wound up being thousands of pages long. I feel like that's sort of the way I approach music, at the nitty-gritty, detail-oriented level. Then I have to work harder to think about it in the larger context. Whereas my friends automatically hear it in the larger context."

When pitches register as individuals with distinct personalities, it's difficult to see the forest for the trees—or the melody for the notes.

8

Dissonant

Despite the adage, scientists studying music have been relentless in their quest to account for taste. It's an enormously complicated question: What makes something enjoyable to listen to?

It's not even clear why we like music at all. Some researchers have speculated that the human tendency to get pleasure out of music is simply a coincidence. Other scientists say that music's ubiquity around the world argues for a genetic component. When musicologists talk about what kinds of music we like, they use two terms we've already discussed a little: *consonance* and *dissonance*.

Even the vocabulary isn't precisely defined. For example, some experts have referred to consonance as the "absence of annoyance."[1] In one 1962 study, John van de Geer, Willem Levelt, and Reinier Plomp, who worked at the Netherlands' Institute for Perception, surveyed people to discover what, exactly, we mean by *consonant* and *dissonant*—but the answers were far from precise.[2] Musicologist David Huron says, "If you just look at the experimental research on consonance and dissonance, we have evidence suggesting that there are at least eleven different phenomena going on here—everything from aspects of the peripheral auditory system and the innervation of nerves in the basilar membrane to enculturation. It spans the whole gamut from detailed physiological issues to familiarization and cultural learning—so the thing to say is that it's an utter mess."

Among the various phenomena related to musical preference, Huron says there is a polarization among scientists about the relative importance of learning and culture and physics and biology in explaining musical preference. These are difficult questions to unravel—whether certain sounds are pleasant to all people and why—and one could write a tome on this subject alone. (Many authors have.) That's not what lies ahead here. We're diving into a few cases of how scientists are studying taste to see what these cases reveal about annoyance.

Even people who grew up in essentially the same circumstances do not respond to all types of music the same way. You might get chills from the piercing wail of an Eddie Van Halen solo, whereas it may take a Wagner aria to tug your brother's heartstrings. When you travel to other parts of the world, the disparities in preferences grow even vaster. Although music is ubiquitous among human cultures, one man's music is another man's noise.

"We fall into this trap of thinking that Western music is music, but there's a pretty amazing variation," says Josh McDermott, the neuroscientist we mentioned earlier for his work with tamarins and music. "Oftentimes, the stuff that people in one part of the world love is just incredibly annoying to us. Some of it is almost unlistenable."

To understand the limits of Western listenability, you might start with some tunes by the Mafa. The Mafa are one of the 250 ethnic groups that make up Cameroon's population. The group originated in the Mandara Mountains, which divide northern Cameroon from Nigeria. The landscape is dry, and the people are mostly farmers, cultivating sorghum, millet, and other crops on terraces on the hilly terrain. The Mafa live throughout the mountains, clustered in small villages of circular homes with thatched roofs. In the extreme north of the mountain range, there is no electrical supply, illness is widespread, and cultural isolation is nearly total.

That's what drew Tom Fritz to the Mandara Mountains. He lives about three thousand miles away in Leipzig, a smallish German city. Among Leipzig's claims to fame is the city's musical history. It is home to Germany's first musical conservatory, and Johann Sebastian Bach worked in Leipzig for nearly thirty years. Fritz is a neurophysicist at the Max Planck Institute for Human Cognitive and Brain Sciences. Fritz is interested in music, which led him to his unlikely relationship with the Mafa.

Fritz's big questions are similar to McDermott's: Is our taste in music learned; is it distinctly human? Does music mean the same thing to different groups of people? He got his hands on some musical recordings from the Mandara Mountains region: it was unlike anything he had ever heard before. "I was astonished by how different their music sounded," Fritz says. "That was one of the main reasons I decided to go visit the Mafa."

Mafa music is produced by a set of different-size flutes played very quickly and repetitively, in complex rhythms. Each flute produces a different note. The flute looks like a long tube with a funnel-shaped mouthpiece, made of clay and wax. Flutes come in different lengths, and it's not a trivial matter to produce sound with the instrument. "You have to invest a lot of energy—it's sort of controlled hyperventilation," says Fritz. He knows what he's talking about. The Mafa gave him a set of flutes as a parting gift, and he has played them back in Leipzig for friends. "It's really exhausting to play."

Most Westerners would likely also find the flute music exhausting to listen to. To us, Mafa music resembles a broken accordion being played by a toddler.

If Mafa music doesn't register as music to Westerners, Fritz wondered how Western music would sound to the Mafa. Specifically, he wanted to know whether the emotional cues that most Westerners take for granted—a minor chord sounding sad or a major chord happy—were recognizable to people who had never heard Western music. The question required finding people with virgin ears for Western tunes, which meant that not just any Mafa farmer in the Mandara Mountains would do.

"You want to go to very remote areas in this Mandara Mountain range . . . and find individuals who have never been to a church before, have never been to a market with an electrical supply, and who, of course, have never listened to a radio," Fritz says. He needed to find the individuals who (often by design) isolated themselves from Westerners. For Fritz, that meant climbing for several hours into the most remote parts of the mountain range. Then he had to convince these folks—who had purposely avoided technology and strangers—to strap on headphones and take part in a foreigner's scientific experiment. It was a tall order.

Across the Atlantic, Josh McDermott was approaching the musical taste question from a different angle. Here was his premise: If people prefer consonant melodies, and consonant melodies are often made of octaves, perfect fifths (those rock power chords), and perfect fourths, perhaps there is something about this arrangement of notes that helps explain our predilection. What's special about perfect fourths and fifths, from a frequency perspective? Maybe there are physical properties of a chord that make it consonant.

When you examine the frequency content of a single note, a pattern emerges. Take the concert pitch A440. This particular A has a fundamental frequency of 440 Hz. That's the main frequency we hear but not the only one. If you play A440 on a piano, you're hearing not only a 440 Hz signal. It's not a pure frequency; the piano produces other frequencies as well. Those other ingredients—called overtones—are integral multiples of that fundamental frequency. For example, a concert A will also include frequencies of 880 Hz and 1,320 Hz, says McDermott. "The frequencies have this precise relationship, and they're spaced regularly in the spectrum." This is called a harmonic sequence.

What about when you play a couple of notes at once to make a chord—how do those frequencies relate to each other? "When the chords are consonant, they also tend to produce frequencies that are harmonically related," says McDermott. The frequencies in consonant chords are mathematically related in the same way that the overtones relate to the fundamental frequency in a single note. In consonant chords, the component frequencies are multiples of each other. "This seems to be the main thing that determines whether people find a chord pleasant or unpleasant."

McDermott's findings suggest that there's something about the human ear and brain that makes an organized, patterned set of frequencies pleasant. These findings also provide an explanation for why dissonant sounds might be unpleasant. Whether this patterned relationship is the only explanation for why we find a chord pleasant isn't clear.

Yet why would a set of pressure oscillations that are mathematically related be music to our ears at all? And is it really true for everyone? McDermott surveyed three hundred people and found that the number of years they spent playing an instrument correlated significantly with how much they preferred consonance over dissonance. If most ears like order, musically trained ears *love* it.

"There's this long debate over whether this is innate or learned from culture," McDermott says. "And it's kind of remained unresolved, in part because it's very hard to do the right kind of cross-cultural studies." Which is exactly what Tom Fritz was attempting to do.

•   •   •

The Mafa in the remote villages were wary of Fritz. He was an outsider with a bizarre request, completely irrelevant to life in the Mandara Mountains. "For the first three weeks, nobody would participate in my experiment," Fritz says. He tried to ingratiate himself and get to know people, which meant consuming "all of these weird millet beers you have to drink if you go and introduce yourself to people." The beer, filled with organisms that a German gut wouldn't ordinarily encounter, poisoned him, but when he tells the story, it doesn't sound as if he minded too much. In addition to drinking the beer, Fritz also learned to play Mafa flutes.

The way Fritz describes it, the Mafa's skepticism eventually melted into amusement. They "decided I was some weird nerd who was engaged in doing completely useless things, like sitting around in a room and not having his own field, but at least seemed not to be dangerous." The Mafa agreed to participate in his experiments. Working with a translator, Fritz asked his participants to listen to recordings of Mafa music and Western piano melodies. He wanted to know whether the Mafa heard emotional content in music and whether their musical preferences matched those of Westerners.

Fritz says that the response to the piano was mixed. Some listeners didn't like the piano, generally. There were two types of listeners: "the innovative listener and the conservative listener. The innovative listener, when he listens to something he never heard before, he might say, 'I've never heard something like that before, but it sounds really nice.' Whereas the conservative listener would rate anything he hadn't heard before as unpleasant."

This may also be a cross-cultural truism: some people expect music to sound a certain way, and when it proves to be something else, they find it unpleasant. In the Mafa's case, the foreign sound of a piano is so out of place that some listeners didn't bother to decide between consonant and dissonant. It was all dissonant to them.

It's hard to keep in mind the number of novelties that were built into Fritz's experiment. None of the participants had heard recorded music before, let alone Western music, let alone a piano. Headphones were alien. "Of course, the listeners were surprised to hear Mafa out of the headphones," Fritz says. "Often, they would turn around and look behind them. Later, they laughed about it and said that at first, they were a little bit scared."

Fritz needed a way to ask his listeners to match a song with a feeling: to do this, he presented the listeners with three photos of a woman. She is smiling in one. She looks sad in another and scared in the third photo. The idea was to have the listeners point out the sad face for sad tunes, the happy face for happy tunes, and so on. "It was the first time, at least for some of them, to see printed-out versions of faces," Fritz says. "Some people were very surprised to see a flat face like that." In fact, Fritz had to exclude several participants because they didn't recognize the printed faces as having any emotional symbolism. A frown didn't symbolize a sad person to some of the Mafa.

Fritz concluded in a paper published in *Current Biology* that for the Mafa, traditional flute music doesn't evoke a range of emotions at all.[3] "For them," Fritz says, "all of their music is somehow happy because all of the music is associated with certain rituals. And even if you have to bury someone, it's still happy music because the music is there so people forget their grief for a while. Their music can do without emotional expressions."

Yet—and this is really intriguing—most Mafa whom Fritz tested heard different emotional content in the Western piano melodies that he played for them. Compared to the Germans whom Fritz studied, Mafa listeners varied more widely in matching emotions with the tunes—but overall, both the German and the Mafa groups performed above chance level. Pieces in a major key were rated as happy; upbeat tempos were also more likely to be associated with the smiling face. Indefinite-mode and low-tempo pieces were more likely to be rated as sad and minor keys as scary. "One thing that I really want to know is how the Mafa can do it," Fritz wonders. "How can they decode those emotional expressions in the music they have never before listened to? What is it that they understand in this? Is it something that goes deeper—something that maybe relates to more abstract patterns of emotional expression that occur in different art forms, maybe even in visual art?" It's an interesting question.

The German group and the Mafa group both preferred consonant pieces to manipulated dissonant versions—these were consonant pieces that had been changed so that their frequencies were out of sync, as in McDermott's study. Fritz and his colleagues wrote that typical Mafa comments were: "You shouldn't let children play the flutes," or "I know this, this is from the people of the Gouzda village. I really don't like how they play the flutes."

Fritz's studies suggest that the preference for consonance (or an aversion to dissonance)—at least, in terms of harmonic order—isn't only a Western thing. Fritz may have an explanation: "I'm quite positive that this relates to the organization of our auditory pathway." He's now looking at how brains process these consonant and dissonant pieces of music. "I find very interesting effects in the auditory pathway," says Fritz. "The consonance seems to be processed more readily than the dissonance."

The suggestion that humans prefer ordered sounds bears on the question of why we dislike other sounds. Take fingernails on a chalkboard, for example. In that screech, the frequencies are random; there is no order.

9

Breaking the Rules

J ust finding the Language Research Center (LRC) at Georgia
State University can be annoying. It's off a two-lane road in
a somewhat undeveloped suburb of Atlanta. There's no sign
out front, just an ordinary black mailbox with white letters on
the side indicating the address.

Turning into the driveway, you are welcomed by a barbed
wire–topped fence with a gate. Again, no sign, only a call box
mounted to the left of the gate. If you're expected, the person who answers the call box will open the gate. From there,
you proceed along a driveway that runs through a copse of
trees. After a quarter mile or so, you arrive at a second barbed
wire–topped fence with another call box. Once again, if you
are expected, someone inside uses a remote control to open

the second gate. Now it's a short drive to a low-slung building with a small parking lot off to the side. The front door of the building is locked, but Sarah Brosnan has the key.

Brosnan is in the psychology department at Georgia State, and she does some of her experimental work at the LRC. The high security is necessary because of threats from animal rights extremists who think that any research with animals is unacceptable, even the benign sort of behavioral research that Brosnan conducts. Some of the more radical animal rights groups have seen fit to firebomb the houses of researchers who use animals in their experiments—thus the locked doors.

Brosnan is interested in social learning in nonhuman primates. In 2003, she published a paper in *Nature* suggesting that capuchin monkeys possessed a notion of fairness, a social concept usually associated exclusively with humans.[1] Her experiments on fairness work like this. Two capuchins will sit in cages next to each other. Their names are Liam and Logan. Liam can see what Logan is up to, and vice versa. Brosnan has taught the monkeys to play a kind of game. She hands them a granite token, and they have to hand it back to her to get a food reward. It's a pretty simple game.

Here's where it gets tricky. There are two food rewards: one is a highly desirable grape, and the other is a considerably less desirable piece of cucumber. In one condition of the experiment, Brosnan hands Liam a token, she holds up a grape, and he hands the token back and gets the grape. Then she hands Logan the token, but instead of the grape, she holds up the piece of cucumber. More often than not, Logan won't hand back the token if he knows his partner got the better reward. Brosnan says that when Logan and his fellow capuchins find themselves in this position of being treated unfairly, their body language lets you know they find this unpleasant. "They tend to turn away—literally turning their backs on you—and move away if they can," says Brosnan.

Since her initial publication in 2003, Brosnan has retreated somewhat from calling the behavior she sees in her capuchins "fairness." Still, she considers the situation analogous to the feeling that humans get when they see someone else getting more pay for doing the same job.

"What we're really testing is how do you respond when you're the one who gets the lower salary," she says, "not how do you respond when you hear there's a discrepancy between salaries in the environment. So the monkeys don't necessarily have to have an ideal of fairness or an idea of the way the world should work. All they have to care about is that they got less than someone else."

Even that interpretation of the result goes too far down the path of anthropomorphizing for some animal behaviorists. Clive Wynne is a psychologist at the University of Florida in Gainesville. He says there's another explanation for what Brosnan is seeing. "There's an older concept, a more basic concept of frustration that humans share with many other species," says Wynne. "It's the tendency to act up if something they were expecting to receive is not given to them." Just as Lucy Fitz Gibbon expects an A to sound like 440 Hz or a conservative listener expects music to sound a certain way, if the monkey expects a better reward and doesn't get it, he's frustrated. "That kind of frustrative behavior is seen in any number of different species," says Wynne. "It was shown back in the 1920s in monkeys."

That work was done by a psychologist at Yale University who had the delicious name of Otto Leif Tinklepaugh. He worked with a species of monkey known as cynomologous and with a particular cynomologous monkey named Psyche. Tinklepaugh's experiment went like this. Psyche would sit in a chair with a board in front of her, preventing her from seeing two cups on a table across the room. When the board was lowered, Psyche could see what the experimenter (Tinklepaugh) was doing. This is how Tinklepaugh recorded the experiment in his notes:

> The experimenter displays a piece of banana, lowers the board and places the banana under one of the cups. The board is then raised, and working behind it, with his hands hidden from the view of the monkey, *the experimenter takes the banana out and deposits a piece of lettuce in its place.* After the delay, the monkey is told to "come get the food." She jumps down from the chair, rushes to the proper container and picks it up. She extends her hand to seize the food. But her hand drops to the floor without touching it. She looks at the lettuce, but (unless very hungry) does not touch it. She looks around the cup and behind the board. She stands up and looks under and around her. She picks the cup up and examines it thoroughly inside and out. She has on occasions turned toward observers present in the room and shrieked at them in apparent anger.[2] [Emphasis in the original.]

Unpredictable, temporary, and unpleasant—the monkey must be annoyed, right? Brian Hare is an anthropologist who is willing to consider the possibility. He leads the Hominoid

Psychology Research Group, which compares the psychology of hominoids (human and nonhuman apes). Hare's graduate student Alexandra Rosati has found another activity that reveals what appears to be a tendency in our primate cousins to become annoyed.

She has done a series of experiments with chimpanzees. She offers the chimpanzee a choice. Option A is a guaranteed couple of peanuts. Chimpanzees are fond of peanuts but not that fond. Not as fond as they are of bananas. It's a cliché, but Rosati says that chimpanzees love bananas. Option B is a chance at a piece of banana—but it's only a chance. There's also a chance that they'll get a chunk of cucumber. Chimpanzees appear to like cucumbers as much as capuchins do; in other words, not much.

No one likes to lose a bet, and chimps, Rosati found, are no exception. When they lose, they try to change their choices, and when they aren't allowed to, they appear to get annoyed. You could call it anger, but it's very different from the anger you see when a chimp is attacked.

Rosati has conducted a similar experiment with bonobos. They, too, appear to get annoyed when they choose the gambling option and lose the bet, and getting a bad outcome made them less likely to choose the risky option on the next trial. The individual bonobos who got most upset at losing were the least likely to choose the risky option overall.

Chimpanzees, on the other hand, didn't seem deterred by losing. They pick the risky option again and again. It seems that for some species, or at least some individuals, the drive to gamble trumps the annoyance of losing.

●   ●   ●

When you think about what's bothering these primates, it can appear, at first glance, to be the road-block kind of annoyance. They have a goal—getting the grapes or the bananas— and the researchers (or bad luck or whatever) are temporarily preventing them from achieving it. Yet there's more to it than that. In the case of the capuchins, they were happy with the cucumbers until the grapes came along. This isn't like being stuck in a traffic jam when you have somewhere else to be. It's more like being cut off by another motorist when you're out for a leisurely drive. Instead of having their plans thwarted, their sense of what was acceptable behavior was thwarted. It was an injustice, albeit minor.

People (and some animals, apparently) face different kinds of annoyances—based on various kinds of unpleasantness. There are annoyances that are physically unpleasant: a skunk smell, fingernails on a chalkboard, flies buzzing in your ear. Another type of annoyance happens when your plans are thwarted: from delayed flights and forms to fill out in triplicate to birds chirping loudly when you're trying to sleep to endless automated phone messages thwarting your desire to talk to your doctor. The third and possibly largest category is made up of annoyances we bring on ourselves, either because they violate certain social rules or conflict with our value system or destroy a reasonable expectation. (Of course, some special annoyances fall into multiple categories—cell phone chatter is a social rule violation and botches your plan to read while you're commuting on the bus.)

An example of this final category comes from Sarah Brookhart, the deputy director of the Association for Psychological Science:

For me, public transportation is teeming with annoyances. Like bacteria on the handrails, the loud one-sided phone conversations about what to have for dinner are part of the deal when you're in a subway car at rush hour. Put on headphones and tune it out. But I could probably ignore a colony of deadly microbes more easily than I can ignore the guy sitting next to me clipping his fingernails. Cranking up the iPod doesn't help. Time stands still. Agonizing suspense after each clip. Has he stopped? Or will there be another click of the teeny guillotine? Then, that unmistakable sound, and a half-moon sliver sails through the air in slow-motion. Worse, I can see it land on the arm of the woman across the aisle; she has no clue, but my skin is crawling with disgust.[3]

Again, there's the disgusting component. Bodily sounds, smells, and pastimes gross us out—perhaps because they seem unhygienic, and there are plenty of evolutionary reasons we'd want to avoid sickness.

Yet there seems to be more going on here. Part of what makes this experience annoying is that Sarah chooses not to clip her fingernails on the subway. This is a value-system trespass. There is no law against clipping your nails on the train. You're expected to be able to put up with that behavior, even though it offends your sensibilities, and this annoys you.

Although breaking social mores seems different from having your tongue burned by a chili pepper, they do have something important in common. For each, there is a thin line between pleasant and unpleasant. An unexpected and minor subversion of your social expectations is also pretty close to the recipe for comedy. Belch loudly at a family barbecue, and you can see for yourself how this works. Everyone in elementary school will probably find this sudden, surprising transgression hysterically funny. Everyone else, annoying. It's this thin line that Hollywood likes to keep a close eye on.

If science has largely ignored the topic of annoyingness, the dramatic arts have not. Movies and plays are filled with annoying characters, meaning that screenwriters and playwrights have to become de facto psychologists. They have to capture the personality traits of what makes someone annoying and put them into a character that everyone will recognize as annoying.

There may seem to be a paradox here. For the most part, we would normally go to great lengths to avoid spending time with someone who is annoying. Yet watching annoying people from a safe distance can actually be tolerable, even amusing. Surely, there is some guilty pleasure to be had from watching Tina Fey get so annoyed that her head is ready to explode.

Playwright Neil Simon and director Gene Saks clearly recognized that possibility when they made the movie *The Odd Couple*, starring Jack Lemmon and Walter Matthau. Matthau played the part of Oscar Madison, a slovenly sportswriter. His New York apartment is a mess. The food in his refrigerator is growing mold. He's divorced, happily so, and is chronically late with his alimony payments.

Jack Lemmon's character, Felix Ungar, is the exact opposite. He's devoted to his wife, even though she kicked him out of the house because of his annoying habits. He makes

strange noises when he clears his throat. He's painfully punc-
tilious and a total neat freak.

The unkempt Madison offers to share his apartment with
pressed-and-creased Ungar after his marriage collapses, but
it's immediately clear that bachelorhood is about the only
thing these two have in common. Ungar offers to do a little
"tidying up" after one of Madison's poker games has left the
apartment a total mess. When the sportswriter wakes up the
next morning, the apartment looks like it's ready for a photo
shoot with *House Beautiful*, the previous night's bacchanalia
a distant memory.

At first, the transformation is pleasing. Even the rumpled
Madison enjoys the laundry service and the home-cooked
meals that Ungar is happy to provide. After a while, though,
the constant dusting and tidying and spraying with air fresh-
ener get to be too much. Madison launches into a tirade. "I
can't take it anymore, Felix, I'm cracking up," says Oscar.
"Everything you do irritates me. And when you're not here,
the things I know you're gonna do when you come in irritate
me. You leave me little notes on my pillow. I told you 158
times I can't stand little notes on my pillow. 'We're all out of
cornflakes. F.U.' Took me three hours to figure out F.U. was
Felix Ungar!" Unger takes all of this in but is equally annoyed
by Oscar's lack of appreciation for his efforts.

> Felix Ungar: I put order in this house. For the first
> time in months, you're saving money. You're
> sleeping on clean sheets. You're eating hot meals
> for a change, and I did it.
> Oscar Madison: Yes, that's right. And then at night
> after we've had your halibut steak and your tartar

sauce, I have to spend the rest of the evening
watching you Saran Wrap the leftovers.

He shakes his head when Madison finishes his tirade with
a complaint about the plate of pasta Unger made for their
dinner.

> Oscar Madison: Now kindly remove that spaghetti
>   from my poker table. [*Felix laughs.*]
> Oscar Madison: [What] the hell's so funny?
> Felix Ungar: It's not spaghetti, it's linguini. [*Oscar
>   picks up the linguini and hurls it against the
>   kitchen wall.*]
> Oscar Madison: Now it's garbage.

The movie is a classic. It's hilarious. Yet both characters
are, in their own ways, totally annoying. Who would want to
watch annoying characters for two hours?

Tom Schulman has an explanation. Schulman is a successful screenwriter. His credits include *Honey, I Shrunk the Kids*
and *Dead Poets Society*. In order to write successful movies,
screenwriters have to get into the heads of their characters.
They capture the essence of human behaviors and translate
them to the screen. So, because the academic world of psychology has largely dropped the ball when it comes to understanding what we find annoying, people like Schulman may
be able to offer some ideas.

"Normally, when we're annoyed with people, we're not
allowed to express it," says Schulman, "especially in public."
Take the experience of sitting on an airplane behind a small
child. The child keeps popping his head over the back of the
seat, hoping for a game of peek-a-boo. Schulman says this is

cute for a while, but he likes to read on airplanes, so the Jack-in-the-box in front of him is an irritating distraction.

"Everybody's watching, and I can't act annoyed," he says. "But in the movie I can laugh when the character gets annoyed." So when Oscar Madison gets annoyed at Felix Ungar in *The Odd Couple* or when Oliver Hardy gets annoyed at Stan Laurel in the Laurel and Hardy movies or when everyone gets annoyed at Newman on *Seinfeld* or when Jackie Gleeson gets annoyed with Art Carney in *The Honeymooners*, we laugh. We can sympathize with the circumstances that are making the character annoyed, and we can laugh because it's not happening to us.

Schulman has written a movie with precisely those qualities. It's called *What about Bob?* and it may be the most rigorous investigation of annoyingness and annoyance ever performed. Bill Murray plays Bob Wiley, a man who is afraid of almost everything. He carries a tissue to open doors because he doesn't want to risk getting germs from the doorknob. He walks up forty flights of stairs because he's too scared to get into an elevator.

Richard Dreyfuss plays Leo Marvin, a self-important psychotherapist who agrees to take Bob on as a patient. Leo is calm, in charge, and the master of his universe. For Bob, in contrast, everything in the world is a challenge.

> Dr. Leo Marvin: Are you married?
> Bob Wiley: I'm divorced.
> Dr. Leo Marvin: Would you like to talk about that?
> Bob Wiley: There are two types of people in this world: Those who like Neil Diamond, and those who don't. My ex-wife loves him.

> Dr. Leo Marvin: [*pause*] I see. So, what you're
> saying is that even though you are an almost-
> paralyzed, multiphobic personality who is in a
> constant state of panic, your wife did not leave
> you, you left her because she . . . liked Neil
> Diamond?

Unlike *The Odd Couple*, the annoyance in *What about Bob?* is asymmetric. In this case, Bob loves Leo. Leo detests Bob. After their initial meeting, Leo tells Bob that he's going away for summer vacation and will meet with him again after Labor Day. Bob is unhinged by this. He needs round-the-clock access to his shrink.

So Bob manages to track down Leo on vacation and wheedles his way into Leo's life. "The Richard Dreyfuss character is a control freak," says Schulman, which has a lot to do with why he finds Bob so annoying. He tries to get rid of Bob, and he can't. "The things that annoy us most are the things that we can't control. I find I'm most annoyed by things when I am in the most controlling of moods."

Schulman says, yes, Bob is annoying. His quirky behavior would make him impossible to live with. His neediness is cloying. He is not someone you'd want to have around for very long. "I think that's true of a lot of movie characters," says Schulman. If people like Bob were in our living rooms, "we wouldn't tolerate them for a second. But on the screen, we root for them because we find the other character they're up against more distasteful."

Schulman says that you have to be careful, though. You don't want to make your annoying character too annoying. He recalls the reaction of the first person who read the script at the studio. "She said, 'I hate this character Bob. Who would want to spend any time around him, much less watch him for two hours on the screen?'" Schulman says he was taken aback.

"I hadn't really thought of that, because I found him somehow lovable in spite of that." More evidence, as if any were needed, that the perception of what's annoying is very subjective. It's a fine line. *What about Bob?* was a successful movie, but there are people who absolutely agreed with that woman at the studio. For those people, it's not only that Bob is unrelentingly annoying, it's that some of us will identify with the character he is tormenting. Leo Marvin may be uptight, but it's hard for some of us to watch him be emotionally eviscerated by Bob.

Screenwriter Mark Silverstein says that to avoid stepping over the too-annoying line, it helps if the characters' annoying behaviors are familiar. "You should recognize someone you know, you should recognize things you do," says Silverstein. He and his writing partner Abby Kohn constructed the character Gigi Phillips for a movie they cowrote called *He's Just Not That into You.* Phillips is looking for love but does it in a way that puts off potential candidates.

For example, Gigi manages to go on a date with a guy who is commitment-phobic. Gigi, on the other hand, "is already talking about her four-year plan," says Kohn, "and where she wants to get married and that she'd like to have a summer house, and they could just like leave their parkas there in the winter and leave their bathing suits there in the summer, and this is where they're going to vacation."

To the guy, Gigi is an irritating nightmare, says Kohn. Yet her yearning for love and marriage makes her sympathetic.

"I think in that way, if you set up a dynamic like that, you can amuse your audience by how much your character is annoying your other character," says Kohn.

In watching that dynamic, Kohn says you can learn more about the character of the annoyee than the annoyer. She says that this realization came from her real-life relationship with Silverstein. They work together in a comfortable office near Hollywood. It's not a large office, though, and they're both in the same room. She says it annoys her when Marc looks over her shoulder while she's writing something. Marc then becomes the annoyer, while she is the annoyee.

"Why is that annoying to me? Is it annoying because I feel him breathing on my neck? Yeah, that's annoying," says Kohn. "Is it annoying because he's too close? Maybe. But maybe what's annoying is I don't quite know the right line yet, and so I'm deleting it five, six, seven times, so I don't want him to read the crappy version before I get it right."

Kohn says that her annoyance comes from her fear that Marc will think less of her for writing crappy versions, but she realizes that annoying behavior can also teach you something about the annoyer. "Cracking your knuckles or talking in a high voice are symptoms of insecurity," she says. "You're nervous, your voice goes up. You're nervous, you start cracking your knuckles. You're nervous, and you tell the same four jokes."

There are also some actors who simply cannot be made annoying onscreen, and that's part of what makes them such successful movie stars, says Silverstein. "Tom Hanks or Julia Roberts, those sort of people. You love them, whatever they're doing." Silverstein says that if you cast Hanks or Roberts as a character who does unlikable things or who is mean to people, the audience will either forgive them or conclude that they must have a good reason for acting so mean.

Sometimes annoying behaviors depicted onscreen can have positive benefits in real life. For example, there's one scene in *What about Bob?* where Bob has weaseled his way into a dinner with Leo Marvin's family at their vacation home. "Bob is making all kinds of 'this is so good' noises," says screenwriter Tom Schulman. "And that just pushes Marvin over the edge." It doesn't sound annoying, but the noises are so excessive and unrelenting that even though they are positive, they become annoying. "That was a habit my wife had, being that demonstrative about the food she was enjoying," Schulman says. "It cured my wife of that habit when she saw the movie."

This seems like a lot of work to extinguish an annoying habit in your spouse, but at the same time, you can't argue with success.

According to University of Louisville psychologist Michael Cunningham, if you want to know why your spouse's habits drive you nuts—such as being too demonstrative about someone else's cooking, for example—you should start by thinking about the immune system, particularly allergies.

Allergies are a good example of the immune system gone awry. Dust is nothing more than a nose-tickler for most people, but people with dust allergies will become severely congested, with constant sneezing and reddened eyes. Or take peanuts. Instead of being a tasty snack, to the person with a peanut allergy they become a deadly menace. Or poison ivy. Some people can frolic barefoot in a patch of poison ivy and be no worse off than if they had walked on a shag carpet. For others, all it takes is a sideways look at the distinctive three-leaved plant, and they break out in an incredibly itchy rash. In addition, when the immune system starts to get things wrong, it doesn't learn from its mistakes. The first exposure to poison ivy can cause a minor rash. Repeated exposure can lead to acute rashes and swelling that may be severe enough to require hospitalization. This heightened reaction with repeated exposure is called sensitization.

Cunningham says that partners are so good at getting under each other's skin because of behaviors that he calls social allergens: small things that don't elicit much of a reaction at first can lead to emotional explosions with repeated exposure. This is the unspoken behavior that gets repeated on an occasional basis—sometimes daily, sometimes less frequently—but packs a bigger and bigger punch with the passage of time.

The idea occurred to Cunningham when he was visiting a colleague. They were having an amiable chat when the phone rang. Cunningham's friend answered the phone, and as the phone conversation progressed, Cunningham watched his friend become agitated. He remained civil, but his face became red. "I could see the irritation, and I knew there must be an issue there."

When the call ended, Cunningham asked what was up. It turns out that the call was from a graduate student who was writing a research paper with Cunningham's friend. The student kept neglecting to make a change that his professor had wanted. "There's nothing more annoying to somebody who is editing a document than to ask for a change and not get it," says Cunningham.

By itself, the dispute was minor. The first time the student failed to make the correction, the professor may hardly have noticed. The second time the response was a bit stronger.

By the third or fourth time, the failure to make the change was causing the professor to become severely agitated and turn red. The professor was not certain whether the student was passively resisting the revision or simply was not paying attention to the comments written in the margin, but neither possibility conveyed respect for the professor's time and effort in providing expert feedback.

The parallel with sensitization was clear. Cunningham has now done numerous studies on social allergens, often as they relate to people in romantic relationships. He says there are four basic categories that most social allergens fall into:

1. *Uncouth habits*. These are behaviors that are not necessarily intended to be annoying but do the trick admirably. Noisy flatulence, nose picking, and knuckle cracking are all examples. Basically, it's anything that a person does that detracts from your physical or sonic space. It's not meant to be intentionally annoying, just as the way that someone who blasts his iPod until you can hear it at the other end of the subway car isn't doing it because he wants to irritate his fellow travelers; he simply likes loud music. "Somebody who plays video games instead of paying attention to the romantic partner who is in the room would also have an uncouth habit," says Cunningham. "People who wear the same clothing from Friday night all the way through to Sunday and don't bother taking a shower all weekend might annoy some partners."

2. *Inconsiderate acts*. Cunningham says that inconsiderate acts are social allergens that do affect a specific individual, but they aren't done with the express intention of annoying that person. For example, you're having a discussion with your partner about a project you find difficult at work. At first, she clucks supportively, but as you explain the nuances of the problem, you notice that she's checking her BlackBerry for any new e-mails. Or your partner is ready to leave the house because you promised to take her out for dinner, and you say, "I'll be ready as soon as this inning is over," and the inning lasts for twenty-five minutes because there are three pitching changes, and she's left standing by the door. Or your partner says she'll pick up the dry cleaning, and she forgets, time after time. Or your partner is chronically late for every appointment you make with him. You get the idea.

3. *Intrusive behaviors*. Unlike the first two categories of social allergens, "intrusive behaviors are intentional and personally directed," says Cunningham. "This is a person who always insists on inflicting his opinion on you, whether you are interested or not. Somebody who tells you how to improve yourself. Gives you unsolicited advice. Just generally tries to dominate you, often with the best of intentions, but you didn't necessarily appoint this person to the role of surrogate parent."

Intrusive behaviors can be relatively anonymous, like the bar bore who insists on telling you what's wrong with America when all you want to do is watch the ballgame. Yet these kinds of behavior can also be quite personal. Parents frequently inflict them on their adult children. Parents know your insecurities best. If you are a successful lawyer, but your mother keeps reminding you that you could have been a doctor, it can get under your skin in a way that's hard for others to appreciate. Or if your spouse is in the habit of reminding you that you don't make as much money as Bob, the boyfriend she left to marry you, this, too, is a good way to set you off.

4. *Norm violations.* "These are intentional behaviors that are not directed at you personally but violate some standard that you have," says Cunningham. "For example, you know somebody who is not paying his income tax. It's not necessarily your business to supervise that person, but you pay your income taxes, and the fact that he doesn't is annoying.

"There are certain norm violations that actually do entail some personal impact; for example, people who violate the building rules about not smoking in the bathroom, and you go into the bathroom right after them, and it stinks. Those norm violations have a personal impact, but it's not directed at you."

Taken together, these four categories of social allergens make living with someone else a challenge. Cunningham likes to recall a scene from the 1999 movie *The Story of Us*:

It's inevitable—suddenly, all you're aware of is that there are too many wet towels on the floor, he's hogging the remote, and he's scratching his back with a fork. Finally, you come face-to-face with the immutable truth that it's virtually impossible to French-kiss a person who takes the new roll of toilet paper and leaves it resting on top of the empty cardboard roll. God forbid, he takes the two seconds to replace it. Does he not see it? Does he not see it?

10

He's Just Not That Annoyed by You

There are people who meet, fall in love, stay married for their entire lives, and never have an unkind word for their spouses. And then there are the other six billion people on the planet.

People frequently describe their partners as both "the love of my life" and "one of the most annoying people I know"—in some cases, the most annoying person they know. It's a baffling paradox. Consider the following scenario. It's a scene that's played out a million times at dinner parties around the world. Think of it as a theme with endless variations.

Four couples are sitting around a table. Everybody is on a second glass of wine. One of the men at the table starts to tell a joke.

"So, three strings go into a bar, and the first string says to the bartender, 'I'd like a Tom Collins, please.'"

At this point, the man's wife interrupts. "Please, not that joke again."

He turns to her. "But they haven't heard it."

She avoids his look. "I have. At least a thousand times."

"But it's funny."

"So you think."

Now the incident has reached a turning point. The guy can finish telling the joke, which will annoy his wife. Or he can stop telling the joke, in which case he'll be irritated.* When they get home, it's easy to imagine the conversation.

"Why do you always interrupt me when I try to tell a joke? When we started dating, you liked my jokes."

"That's all you ever do at dinner parties. Tell jokes. We were talking about politics, and you pipe up with your dumb joke about strings."

"Why do you always have to interrupt me at dinner parties? Can't you ever let me finish a thought in public? Can't you let other people decide what they do or don't want to hear?"

And so on.

---

*The bartender says, "We don't serve strings here. Get out." The second string goes up to the bartender and says, "A Bloody Mary, please." The bartender says, "Didn't you hear what I told your friend? We don't serve strings here. Get out." Seeing this, the third string goes into the bathroom, unravels his ends, and ties himself in a bow. Then he goes out to the bar and says to the bartender, "I'd like a martini, please, straight up, with a twist." The bartender looks at him suspiciously. "Are you a string?" he asks. "No, I'm a frayed knot."

A reasonably well-adjusted couple will weather this contretemps. For a troubled marriage, it could take them one step closer to the end. Diane Felmlee has thought a lot about the circumstances that bring couples to this predicament. She's a sociologist at the University of California, Davis. After decades of research, she's convinced that she knows what's going on.

The answer first occurred to her in the 1980s when she was just starting her academic career at Indiana University in Bloomington. She even remembers the day. She was having lunch with some of her women friends when the conversation turned to relationships. The women were sharing complaints about their partners. "One woman was saying her husband was never there on the weekends," Felmlee recalls. "He was always working so hard, and she wished he was around more. So I asked her what drew her to him in the first place."

Felmlee says her friend replied that she and her husband had been high school sweethearts, and what had first impressed her about him was that he was an incredibly hard worker. "It was clear he was going to be one of the more successful people in the class," Felmlee remembers her friend saying. "Another woman said that her fiancé never talked with her about his feelings. 'He won't tell me what's bothering him.' So I asked her, 'What drew you to him?' and she said, "Well, he had this cool about him, a kind of cool demeanor.' And I'm thinking, 'Cool, reserved men don't emote. They're not going to talk about their feelings.'"

Felmlee says that she saw a pattern. In each case, it seemed that the very quality that was initially attractive became an irksome characteristic later in the relationship. Were her friends unusual, or was this a common occurrence? Felmlee decided to investigate. At the time, she was teaching a big lecture class. College sophomores are a common proving ground for new psychological theories, so it only made sense for her to engage her class. "I just had them pull out a piece of paper and asked them to think of their boyfriend or girlfriend and then write down what first attracted them to that person."

Now, when you are the teacher, and you ask your class a question, you run a high risk of getting the answers your students think you want to hear. So she then asked a few unrelated questions to disguise what she was getting at. "And then I asked them what they least liked about that person. And if their relationship had ended, I asked why it ended."

The answers confirmed her initial suspicions. It was fairly common for the students to be turned off by the very thing that first attracted them to the person they were—or had been—dating. In the last few decades, Felmlee has been conducting studies with couples to further explore this problem of what she calls "fatal attractions." She says that virtually any positive trait that you can name can also be looked at as an annoyance.

"We asked one guy what he liked about a former girlfriend, and he listed every part of this woman's body, including the most intimate parts. And when he answered the question 'Why did you split up?' he said that the relationship was based only on lust. There wasn't enough love. I thought, 'Well, he got what he wanted initially. Now he's not happy with it.'" Similarly, Felmlee remembers a woman in one of her studies who really liked her husband's body, and then she complained that he was always working out, instead of spending time with her.

The list goes on. Felmlee says that someone who is seen as humorous at the start of a relationship can later be considered "flaky" or "immature." One woman reported that she was attracted by her boyfriend's sense of humor, but then she complained that he "doesn't always take other people's feelings seriously (jokes around too much)."

Caring is another positive quality with a downside. Felmlee reports that one woman was attracted to a man who was "very attentive" and persistent, but she disliked that he "tries to be controlling." Another woman described a former partner as "caring," "sensitive," and someone who listened to her. Yet she did not like the fact that he also got jealous very easily, and "he hated it when [she] wanted to spend time with other friends."[1]

For nearly every positive quality that you can think of, there's a flip side that can become annoying over time:

- People who are nice and agreeable can later be seen as passive and prone to letting people walk all over them.
- Someone who is strong willed and knows where he is going can later appear stubborn and unreasonable.
- The outgoing, garrulous life of the party can become the nonstop performer who won't shut up.
- The solicitous, caring suitor becomes the clingy, needy partner.
- An exciting risk taker turns into an irresponsible parent.
- The physically attractive love interest becomes the high-maintenance spouse.
- Laid-back turns into lazy.
- A successful person becomes a workaholic.

In a way, the concept of fatal attraction bears a resemblance to hedonic reversal but backward. With relationships, we start off finding a quality of our mates attractive, and over time it becomes annoying. With hedonic reversal, something that is intrinsically unpleasant—like eating hot chili peppers—becomes enjoyable with repeated exposure. This is not only an American phenomenon. Felmlee has tested people all over the world, and the same pattern seems to hold.

The other thing she consistently finds is that the more strongly someone exhibits a particular trait, the more likely that trait is to become annoying. Again, the dose matters. So, for example, a spouse is more likely to become annoyed with a partner who is exceptionally funny and always telling jokes than with one who makes a witty remark on occasion.

What's going on here? Why do strengths become weaknesses and endearing qualities, irritants? "I call it disillusionment," says Felmlee. She believes the answer may be related to something called social exchange theory. "Extreme traits have rewards," she says, "but they also have costs associated with them, especially when you are in a relationship."

Take independence. "Independence can be valued in a partner, one who can stand on his own two feet," says Felmlee. "But if you're too independent, that means you don't need your wife. And that can have costs in a relationship."

Felmlee has thought a lot about how couples might get around some of these points. Self-awareness helps. She recalls one man who complained that his wife was stubborn. "On the other hand, what he really liked about her and loved from the beginning was her strength of character. And he said he was entirely committed to her and planned to be with her for the rest of his life." This man, at least, seemed to be aware that positive qualities have an inherent downside. "And he seemed aware of his own limitations. He said, 'I'm stubborn, too, and she has to put up with that.'"

"It's not like you get this perfect person, and there are no downsides to his or her qualities," says Felmlee. "It just doesn't happen."

The other thing that can create annoyance in relationships is repetition. Even if your partner only occasionally leaves a clump of hair in the drain or talks while he's eating, spending a lifetime with someone creates ample opportunities for repeated exposure. "The same thing keeps happening over and over and over again in a marriage," says Elaine Hatfield, a psychologist at the University of Hawaii and a fiction writer to boot, "because we all have our goofy little quirks." Anything can become annoying with time, but Hatfield says that these annoyances get amplified according to the principles of something called equity theory.

The idea is that individuals and groups are encouraged to behave fairly with one another, and that people are most comfortable when they feel they are being treated equitably. Equity theory says that if you feel you are in an inequitable relationship, you will try to change that by restoring psychological or actual equity or by leaving the relationship. If the equity balance tilts toward you, and you're getting a good deal in a relationship, then you might be willing to ignore your partner's annoying habits and do less dishing out of things that get his goat. "But if you think, 'That guy, he takes advantage of me at every turn, I'm stuck here with the eight children, I cannot leave, and he's out having a great time,' it would just grate on you more," says Hatfield.

Hatfield's relationship with her own husband validates this theory. She says that nothing her husband does annoys her. Really. She feels that their relationship is in excellent balance, and she is truly grateful that a person as wonderful as he is loves her. It's almost as if Hatfield can't imagine being annoyed with her husband. Her lack of irritation with him is not because Hatfield is an easygoing person who never gets annoyed with anyone. "I get so mad at some people in my life, I would happily have them die," she says with a tone of slightly bemused exaggeration.

There could be more than mere repetition at stake here, says Michael Cunningham, the scientist who came up with that list of social allergens.

First, when a relationship starts and partners are in that dreamy love state, the other person is seen through rose-tinted glasses. It's not that you're unaware of your partner's annoying habit of cracking his knuckles; it's just that it doesn't seem like a big deal. Later on, when what Cunningham calls deromanticization has taken place, the willingness to overlook these uncouth behaviors evaporates. And things can only get worse. "You might have said something to your partner, and he promised to make a change," says Cunningham. "But then the change didn't happen, which conveys a certain attitude of disrespect or indifference."

The second reason these social allergens become more annoying with time is that they occur more frequently after the initial romantic blast. Cunningham says that psychologist Rowland S. Miller has a good explanation why:

> Once a courtship is over and a partner has been
> won, people usually relax their crafting of their

self-presentations and try less hard to make consistently favorable impressions on those from whom acceptance is assured. . . . When we can rely on others' approbation and approval, we stop trying so hard to get them to like us. Thus, it is that a suitor who never appeared for breakfast without his beard well-trimmed and his cologne apparent becomes a spouse who shows up in his underwear, unwashed and unshaven, and then steals the last doughnut.[2]

Men and women differ on which social allergens they're most likely to exhibit and which ones are the most likely to bug them. Men tend to see women as inconsiderate, intrusive, and increasingly domineering and controlling as a relationship progresses. Perhaps not surprisingly, women see men as more likely to exhibit uncouth behaviors. Women were more annoyed than men were with violations of societal expectations, such as smoking in no-smoking areas or ignoring parking tickets.

One thing most couples have noticed is that the same behavior that drives you crazy when your partner does it can be (relatively) easy to ignore when someone outside the relationship does it. Cunningham says there are two reasons for this. One is that if it's not your partner, you believe you are going to escape it. You can get through any dinner sitting next to an annoying person because you know that eventually it will be over—and you don't have to wonder when. It ends when you leave the dinner table. Yet if your spouse has that same annoying trait, it will be present that night and at lunch the next day and on and on and on. The other reason is that you know you can expect irritating behaviors out in the big, bad world.

"When you're out in public, you put the Teflon on," says Cunningham. "But with spouses, you may have the shields down, and they may get to you more easily." When you are at home, you hope to have a comfortable environment with agreeable people. "Outside in the world, you expect to deal with irksome people," says Cunningham. It's a case of fore-warned is forearmed.

So what can you do? How can you prevent these social allergens from destroying your relationship? "The most com-mon thing to do is to avoid the other person," says Cunning-ham. This is not necessarily a good thing for relationships, "but it does explain separate bedrooms, separate vacations, and things."

Even though this advice is likely to have the same effect on you as the phrase "eat more fruits and vegetables," Cun-ningham says you should try to be accepting of your part-ner's irritating habits. "This trait is a part of this person," he says. "You've got to take this if you want all of the other good things."

A slightly more practical approach is to try to reclassify behaviors. "Some people have said that you can see certain quirks that used to be annoying as actually endearing," says Cunningham. Unfortunately, this reclassification usually occurs posthumously. Your spouse's infuriating habit of snapping his bubblegum may seem oddly charming when the poor guy is remembered at his funeral. "If you can do that before the per-son has passed on, you're ahead of the game." Cunningham also notes that some people asked their spouse to cease and desist the annoying behavior, but that was effective in only a minority of cases, because some allergens were unintentional and hard to control and others were actions the offender felt entitled to perform.

Of course, we may be missing an angle here. There are times when, either consciously or unconsciously, we want to annoy our partners, says psychologist Arthur Aron of the State University of New York in Stony Brook. Aron says that sometimes we realize we are trying to get back at our partners for some transgression, and spouses know best what will get their partners' goat. "You know when you hang out with someone, don't bring up certain topics, or, if you do, don't push it too hard," says Aron. "With spouses, we know that our partners know our hot buttons, and it's even more annoying when our partners bring them up."

Intentionality of action may factor significantly in the annoying quotient. A door slammed by the wind is way less annoying than a door slammed by an angry spouse. Aron believes that this intentional "pushing too hard" isn't limited to adult relationships. "Kids do this a lot with their parents. And to some extent, parents with their kids." Aron says that children will deliberately not clean up their rooms, will drink milk directly from the container, and will not hand in their homework as a way to annoy a parent who sets a curfew too early or refuses to raise an allowance. Like Hatfield, Aron believes that many of these annoyances will be overlooked when there is commitment in a relationship and will be exaggerated when there is not. Growing annoyance can be a sign of trouble to come.

The good news here is that there are ways to address the problem. Aron says that one of the most important things you can do in a relationship is celebrate when something good happens to your partner. "That's even more important than supporting him or her when things go bad," says Aron.

Another trick is to be sure to do novel, challenging, exciting things with your partner, fairly often. Anything you can do that will make your relationship better will tend to make your partner less annoying. It's a case of a familiar aphorism turned on its head: "Mind the pounds, and the pennies will take care of themselves."

Just as you might fall for a person with one trait and then find that you're annoyed by the same trait years later, the same can happen in the workplace. An employer may hire someone for a characteristic that later turns out to be annoying.

Robert Hogan has some ideas about that. In fact, he's made a career of convincing companies that he can weed out the undesirable hires or at least give those people feedback that might help them change their behavior. One look at his house on Amelia Island on the Atlantic Coast of Florida is enough to tell you that he's made a pretty successful career out of it. Amelia Island is an enclave of wealth and privilege. Hogan describes himself as "one of two liberals on the island." His house sits at the edge of a tidal wetland on the island's west coast. An unmemorable exterior gives way to a spectacular modern interior, with soaring ceilings, huge windows looking over the wetlands, and walls intersecting at interesting angles. This splendid home is where Hogan remotely runs Hogan Assessment Systems, Inc., a management consultant business located in Tulsa, Oklahoma, that was founded by Hogan and his wife, Joyce, when they were both professors at the University of Tulsa.

Hogan is a personality psychologist. "The problem with personality psychology as a discipline is that it started with Freud and Jung and Adler and Erikson," he says. "They set the field off in the wrong direction. They argued that the most important generalization you can make about people is that everyone was somewhat neurotic, which means the big problem of life is to overcome your neurosis. Which means the goal of psychological assessment is to identify the sources of your psychopathology. That whole thing was a total mistake."

The reason it was a mistake, according to Hogan, is that Freud and Jung and Adler were all crazy, to use the nontechnical term. They assumed that their own craziness was simply a version of what everybody else suffered from. "The trick is to get an impartial perspective on human nature so that you can get your own biography out of the way," says Hogan. "It goes back to Socrates, 'Know thyself.' I always thought when I was young that 'Know thyself' was Freudian. Know the secret you that's inside you."

That's not what he thinks anymore. "For Socrates and the Greeks, self-knowledge had to do with knowing the limits to your performance capabilities," he says. "Basically, knowing what you're good at and not good at. The best data for that are what other people are going to say about you." In other words, what you think of yourself is irrelevant. If everybody you come in contact with thinks you're a jerk, you're a jerk whether you think that or not. "The you that you know is hardly worth knowing because you made it up," says Hogan. "We're all the stars in our own little dramas." In other words, annoying people probably have no idea how annoying they are.

Hogan was also interested in the question of leadership. "Because to take leadership seriously means you have to take personality seriously," he says. As he looked through the psychology literature, he found little consensus on what makes a good leader. So he turned the question on its head and asked, What makes a bad leader? There are a lot of bad leaders out there, says Hogan. A senior manager at one of the nation's largest retailers estimates that two-thirds of the managers they hired were bad. "Here are the reasons they failed," says Hogan. "They were arrogant, abrasive, and neurotic."

So Hogan looked at personality disorders that characterized people who were arrogant, abrasive, and neurotic and "did some recreational psychometrics and boom—up pops this test, and it just works like crazy in predicting performance," he says. "We don't like to talk about personality disorders because lawyers will come after us." To be a good leader, however, you have to get along.

There are approximately 165 questions in the Hogan Leadership Challenge test. The test taker is asked to "agree" or "disagree" with questions like, "I could do a better job running the country than the people doing it now," "I am popular at parties," "I care what people think of me," and "I like to wear costumes."

Hogan has come up with eleven different scales that reflect someone's management strengths or, more important, his or her weaknesses: excitable, cautious, skeptical, reserved, bold, mischievous, colorful, imaginative, diligent, and dutiful. To set up the scoring, he asked managers to rate one another on each of these scales. He did this for thousands of people, compiling information that he stores in a database back at company headquarters.

Then he administered his test to these same managers and correlated the answers that the managers gave on the test with what people said about them. How a person answered a specific question is not important. The pattern of the answers provides the clues to what kind of person he or she is. So, for example, people who agree with the statements "I am popular at parties" and "I like to wear costumes" but disagree with the statements "I could do a better job running the country than the people doing it now" and "I care what people think of me" might be more likely to be judged as high on the colorful scale and low on the diligent scale. The key point is that Hogan did not start off with any predictions about how "a colorful" person would answer the questions. He simply measured the answers and correlated them with the ratings given by others.

Just as with chili peppers, intensity seems to be the issue here. Colorful and imaginative could mean that you'd be good at running a design department, or it might indicate that you're building a bomb shelter to wait out a potential alien invasion. Dutiful and diligent could mean that you inspire your coworkers with your work ethic, or you might be an officious pencil pusher with a penchant for correcting grammar and punctuation.

If you realize that you're trending too far on the intensity scale, is there anything you can do about it? "There are two general answers to that," says Hogan. "First is that you can't get better at it unless you know what you're doing. So, some feedback is absolutely essential." The second answer is that some people can modify their behavior to be more effective managers and concomitantly less irritating. Others can't.

Hogan draws an analogy with sports. "Good athletes are coachable," he says. "There are lots of really talented guys who are not coachable, and they don't make out." Take the case of tennis player Andy Roddick. "Roddick turned out to be coachable," says Hogan. He signed on a new coach named Larry Stefanki. Stefanki found flaws in Roddick's form and told him how to fix them. "He became the hottest guy on the [pro tennis] tour, but it's only because he grew up enough that he's willing to listen to some feedback," says Hogan. "There's this whole positive psychology movement in America right now where the notion is to ignore your deficits and focus on your positives. That's just suicide. There's no news in good news. You can only improve your game by getting feedback on what you're doing wrong, and being irritating is one thing people do wrong."

Is it possible to come up with a shorthand test, one that simply measures how annoying someone is? Hogan says yes, and here are the items he'd use.

The Annoying Inventory

Irritable

- Other people often annoy me.
- I find there are few people I can really trust.
- I don't mind criticizing people when they deserve it.
- People often disappoint me.
- My moods can change quickly.
- These days people seem to have forgotten what hard work actually is.
- I must admit, I am sometimes hard to please.

Arrogant

- I insist on receiving the respect I am due.
- In time, people will appreciate my talents.

- I am better at what I do than almost anyone.
- I enjoy being the center of attention.
- Other people can often sense my power.
- Other people find me attractive.
- When I want to, I know how to turn on the charm.

Picky

- If you want something done right, you need to do it yourself.
- When I am irritated, I let people know.
- I have very high standards for work performance.
- I don't really care what other people think of me.
- When people work for me, I supervise them closely.
- It is important to pay attention to the details at work.

Why these statements? Hogan says that he pulled them out of his hat (actually, he used a more colorful expression), but that's only partly true. As someone who has been developing personality surveys for decades, Hogan now has an almost innate sense of what kinds of questions will pinpoint the various types of personalities. Although it may seem a little hit-or-miss, this is how most new survey instruments are developed.

Hogan's initial thought was to have people respond to each statement with either "agree" or "disagree," but Paul Connolly had a different idea. Connolly is the president of Performance Programs, a company that uses Hogan surveys in its work with corporate human resource departments. Connolly says that the test would be more informative if there were a 5-point scale: 5 means you strongly agree with the statement, 1 means you strongly disagree.

From June 16 to June 30, 2010, Hogan slipped these statements into his development survey, and as a result,

2,399 people were unwitting test subjects who assessed the usefulness of what we'll call the Hogan Annoying Inventory (HAI). The initial data show several important things. First, there was a good spread of responses on each statement. If everybody had responded "strongly agree" to the statement "It is important to pay attention to details at work," it wouldn't be a very good statement for separating annoying from not-annoying people. The other thing the first data show is that the responses correlate with other qualities that the Hogan survey measures. According to this initial sample, an annoying person is pretty neurotic, pretty impulsive, and quite outgoing and talkative. In other words, a poorly adjusted extrovert. Yeah, that sounds about right.

It's hard to know whether the HAI really measures someone's annoyingness. Validating any new inventory is tricky, says Georgine Pion, a psychologist at Vanderbilt University. One way is to have a panel of experts rate people for how annoying they are and then give them the HAI and see how well the results compare with the expert ratings. There are problems with this approach, however. You have to get a group of people who are willing to be judged for how annoying they are. Or you can lie to people and tell them you are actually measuring something else and hope to heck they never find out the truth. Then there's the problem of choosing the expert. There are no "experts" to choose from, in part because annoyingness is so subjective, and in part because it's a young scientific field.

Pion says that another approach is to ask people to evaluate the statements in the survey. For example, how annoying would someone be if she possessed the trait "My moods can change quickly"? That was easier to start with, so on

July 26, 2010, 265 people were e-mailed a survey that included a list of traits based on the HAI and were asked how annoying people with those traits would be on a scale from not annoying at all to extremely annoying. A total of 134 people returned the survey. The trait that people found most annoying on average was "People who think they are better at what they do than almost anyone." Surprisingly, the least annoying trait was judged to be "People who have very high standards for work performance."

Some curious things emerged from these two efforts to validate the HAI. Even though "People who think they are better at what they do than almost anyone" was considered an annoying trait, the related statement "I am better at what I do than almost anyone" showed almost no correlation with whether people thought of themselves as annoying.

People find arrogance annoying, but the arrogant don't think of themselves as annoying. On one level, that's not surprising: arrogant people think only good things about themselves. Still, here's what this really seems to mean: people who are annoying don't realize they're annoying.

The statement that most closely tracked with self-ratings of annoyingness was "When I want to, I can turn on the charm." Yet that same trait, "People who can turn on the charm," was not regarded as annoying in the pilot study.

The survey suggests something that most of us probably suspect intuitively: it's really hard to know whether you're annoying, and if you do annoy someone, it's extremely hard to figure out why.

11

Better Late Than Never Doesn't Apply Here

Ifaluk is a coral atoll in the Yap State of the Federated States of Micronesia. It's one of the Caroline Islands. Never heard of it? Not surprising. It's tiny. Its land mass is about half the size of Central Park in New York City. Approximately six hundred people live there.

It rains a lot in Ifaluk, something in the neighborhood of one hundred inches per year, about three times the average for Seattle. Every so often a typhoon sweeps by, flattening the island. Ifaluk isn't easy to get to. Looked at another way, it isn't easy to leave.

So, let's say you were a psychologist interested in studying annoyance, and you wanted to create a pressure cooker of a situation where the conditions were challenging, the population fixed, and the opportunities for escape negligible. It sounds as if Ifaluk might be your natural laboratory. Yet when anthropologist Catherine Lutz visited Ifaluk in the late 1970s, she found something remarkable. No one seemed to be annoyed about anything. Not just a few serene people. Everyone. All the time. Calm as could be. And it wasn't because annoyances didn't exist. They abounded. How could this be? How can conditions that would surely be insanely annoying to an American not trouble the residents of Ifaluk one tiny bit?

Lutz's explanation is that emotions are shaped by culture. Most of the time, we tend to think of emotions as something we're born with. Lutz, however, believes that this is not the right way to think about emotions. She says that they are set by the way we are raised and by the expectations that are placed on us from day one. What's more, emotions are not so much individual traits but properties that emerge from communities, from interactions with other people. According to this idea, you don't typically have emotions in isolation. "One person's anger (*song*) entails another's fear (*metagu*); someone's experiencing grief and frustration creates compassion/love/sadness (*fago*) in others," wrote Lutz about the Ifaluk islanders.[1]

So, rather than show anger or frustration or annoyance, the people of Ifaluk use their words to express their feelings. They have a rich vocabulary to express a variety of states of annoyance. There's *tipmochmoch*, the annoyance that comes with feeling ill. There's *lingeringer*, the annoyance that builds from a series of minor but unwanted events. There's *nguch*, the annoyance with relatives who do the Ifaluk equivalent of failing to show up for a holiday dinner. Best of all, there's *tang*, which Lutz describes as the frustration that occurs "in the face of personal misfortunes and slights which one is helpless to redress."

Another important word for communicating annoyance is *song*. It's what Lutz calls justifiable anger. Basically, it means, "You've done something that pisses me off. I know it, and you know it. But because expressing that annoyance would be inappropriate, I'll let it go, and so will you." It's sort of a twist on the Western concept of forgive-and-forget, but it's more like not-forgive-and-forget.

Lutz wasn't the first to uncover a society where annoyance was anathema. In the 1960s, an anthropologist named Jean Briggs spent more than a year with the Utkuhikhalingmiut* Eskimos in northern Canada. She persuaded one of the families to essentially adopt her so that she could experience, as well as study, the culture.

Like the Ifaluk, the Utkuhikhalingmiut frowned on expressions of negative emotion. Indeed, someone who showed even a trace of annoyance faced silence, loneliness, and rejection— something Briggs learned the hard way. She made the mistake of saying something to a fisherman who had damaged an Utkuhikhalingmiut fishing net. She had to endure months of the silent treatment, a distressing experience.

The notion that emotions are shaped by culture is becoming widely accepted by people who study such things, and it explains a lot about why Americans find people from other countries annoying, and vice versa.

---

*Pronounced Utkuhikhalingmiut.

• • •

Hazel Rose Markus is a psychologist at Stanford University and the director of the Center for Comparative Studies in Race and Ethnicity. In 1991, she and Shinobu Kitayama wrote a seminal paper titled "Culture and the Self: Implications for Cognition, Emotion, and Motivation." In it, they said,

> In America, "the squeaky wheel gets the grease." In Japan, "the nail that stands out gets pounded down." American parents who are trying to induce their children to eat their suppers are fond of saying "think of the starving kids in Ethiopia, and appreciate how lucky you are to be different from them." Japanese parents are likely to say "Think about the farmer who worked so hard to produce this rice for you; if you don't eat it, he will feel bad, for his efforts will have been in vain." . . . A small Texas corporation seeking to elevate productivity told its employees to look in the mirror and say "I am beautiful" 100 times before coming to work each day. Employees of a Japanese supermarket that was recently opened in New Jersey were instructed to begin the day by holding hands and telling each other that "he" or "she is beautiful."

Markus and Kitayama argue that these contrary points of view help illuminate a fundamental difference in how Eastern and Western cultures conceive of what psychologists call "self." Your concept of self determines how you perceive and respond to your environment.

In the Western world—at least, in the parts of the Western world that Markus has studied—you are supposed to be in control of your environment. "You think about yourself as independent, separate from others," says Markus. "You should be in charge of your actions, you should be freely making choices, and you should be influencing your world. Control is key. And when you can't have that kind of influence over your environment, over other people, over your world, it's very irritating and annoying, because that's what you should be doing, to be a good self."

On the other hand, according to Markus, Japanese and other Asian cultures have an interdependent concept of self. Rather than being unique, solitary individuals who are out for what is best for them and them alone, they see themselves as a node in a network. The sense of self is less individualistic and more collective.

Markus's coauthor Shinobu Kitayama has lived in both cultures and has an acute appreciation of how these different views of self govern behavior. Kitayama is now a professor at the University of Michigan. He says that Americans think nothing about walking down a public street talking on their cell phones, no matter how annoying that behavior might be to others. "That's inconceivable in Eastern cultures," he says. He was reminded of this on a recent trip back to Japan. While he was waiting for a flight home, he went into the lounge for Northwest Airlines (as it then was known) and pulled out his cell phone to make a call. "People got very upset," he recalls.

A survey conducted by the Association of Japanese Private Railways, and translated by Reuters, provides more evidence.[2] The 2009 findings, which drew from 4,200

survey respondents, indicated that the top four annoyances on trains were:

1. Noisy conversation, horsing around
2. Music from headphones
3. The way passengers sit [particularly, if you take up
   more than your fair share of space]
4. Cellphone ringtones and talking on phone.

Perhaps the most foreign top annoyance was number 6:
"applying make-up." All of these behaviors draw attention to
the person or do not perpetuate the common good. In Japan,
separating yourself from the pack is annoying. In America,
it's a virtue. Kitayama says that people in a collectivist culture
learn early on that fitting in is an important life skill. He says
that there are data showing that Asian teenagers tend on average to be less annoyed with their parents, because their parents are part of their concept of self. So, being annoyed with
one's parents is tantamount to being annoyed with oneself.

There is experimental evidence for this notion that various
cultures have different self-identities. For example, in one
study, researchers showed subjects a group of five cartoon
characters in a row, but one of the characters was clearly in
the foreground, the others slightly behind. The characters all
had expressive faces, and it was easy to infer their emotional
states. The participants in the experiment were supposed to
judge the mood of the person in the foreground.

For Americans, all of their attention was on the foreground
character. You could see that in the way their eyes moved as
they took in the scene. Their gaze was fixed on the foreground
character, with scarcely a glance at those on either side. They

judged the mood of the foreground character without refer-ring to the others in the picture.

When the same picture was shown to experimental sub-jects from a more collectivist culture, their eye movements revealed a different pattern. Their eyes flitted around, taking in the entire scene. They judged the scene from a holistic per-spective. If the people in the background were sad or frown-ing, then the smiling figure in the center was rated less happy than an American would rate that figure. If the people in the background were smiling, the mood of the central character was judged to be even more positive than if the background expressions were neutral.

Phoebe Ellsworth is a psychology professor at the University of Washington. She has conducted a number of experiments along these basic lines. She says that the difference reflects the way the Japanese are brought up and how they create their sense of self. They have a hard time detaching the indi-vidual from the group, something that Americans do without a second thought.

If something good happens to an American, chances are that person will simply feel good about it. If the same good thing happens to people from a collectivist culture, Ellsworth says, the individuals are likely to feel that it's not going to last or that their friends are going to envy them for their success, so they have to guard against being boastful. "Americans can-not stretch their minds to think that anything negative could occur in a happy situation," says Ellsworth.

The Japanese emotion called *amae* is another example of cultures shaping annoyance. "It's a state of happy dependence," says Ellsworth. The closest parallel in Western culture is in the relationship between mother and child. The child can pester the mother and disturb her when she's working, and when the mother doesn't get annoyed, we feel good because it shows what a close relationship it is. In Japan, this tolerance is not limited to a child's behavior. It can include circumstances involving adults, in which one person can break a few social rules, understanding that the other person will tolerate it because they have such a close relationship. "We did a study where people asked for favors," says Ellsworth. "Japanese subjects who participated in the study were much more willing to tolerate an inappropriate request for a favor from somebody and even to see that as a good thing."

Here is the kind of scenario that researchers used to study *amae*. They asked subjects whether they would be annoyed by a neighbor who asked them to water his plants while he was away. Most people said that wouldn't be annoying. Then, however, they asked the subjects what if the trip were for a week, would that be annoying? What about a month? Six months? A year? "The Americans got annoyed much sooner," says Ellsworth. "They would see this as an inappropriate trespass on their goodwill at maybe one week. The Japanese would eventually see it as too much of an imposition, but the favor would have to be much bigger before they got to that point. We value independence, and we have contempt for people who seem too dependent."

Yet if Americans get annoyed with the Japanese for seeming to be self-effacing and unreasonably tolerant, the flip side of that helps explain why other cultures are irritated by Americans. "What annoys people about Americans is that we have these big cheesy smiles on our faces all of the time, for no apparent reason whatsoever," says Stanford University's Hazel Markus. "For an American, a smile says, 'I'm okay, I'm a good person, I'm in control, and I'm worth knowing.' Everybody else thinks, 'What's the matter with this person? Is this person insane? Why do they have this smile on? They don't know me, why are they smiling at me?'" In other words, the smile is annoying. "They think it's fake, and along with that, what they find really annoying is that Americans act like they're your best friend after five minutes."

If you go to Amazon.com, you can purchase three DVDs of the movie *Avatar* for $59.97. If you go to a Web site that specializes in merchandise from China, you can buy a hundred copies of that film for $140. The U.S. government has waged a legal war by means of the World Trade Organization to crack down on this practice, but psychologists say that even if they win the legal war, they may be fighting a cultural difference that will be hard to overcome. Michael Ross of the University of Waterloo and Qi Wang from Cornell University have looked into how a culture's history shapes its present attitudes.[3] They point to research that demonstrates the Chinese tendency to accept ancient wisdom as valid. By contrast, Western tradition encourages authors to "question, alter, and reject earlier ideas and theories."

Think of Westerners' concept of plagiarism. "Western plagiarizers typically claim lack of intent and apologize, resign, or pay damages. In China, such 'borrowing' of past work does not engender the same level of social disapproval," Ross and Wang wrote. "The East Asian emphasis on the interconnectedness of selves implies that what is yours is also mine. I don't have to apologize for appropriating your words and thoughts as if they were my own. Indeed, my use of your words demonstrates my admiration for you. In the West, with its clear demarcation between mine and yours, similar actions seem more akin to theft than admiration." At least legally, China has started to move away from this attitude by beginning to accept international norms about copyrighted material, but this psychological point of view helps explain why the change has been infuriatingly slow to Western publishers.

Historical attitudes aren't the only thing that raises barriers and creates cross-cultural annoyances. Another problem occurs when dissimilar cultures have different perceptions of time.

Consider this example. Today, Neil Altman is a psychotherapist in New York City. As a young man, Altman went to India as a Peace Corps volunteer, where he helped implement some new agricultural practices. Every so often, he had the occasion to visit the local horticulture office to get seeds and the like. The seeds were dispensed by the man who ran the office, Mr. Kahn, so Altman's first stop was at Mr. Kahn's desk. Inevitably, there would be six or eight people sitting around the desk, presumably also there to get seeds or transact some other business.

Altman describes what transpired this way:

> Altman: "Good morning, Mr. Kahn, could I get some tomato seeds, please?"
> Kahn: "Good morning, Volunteer sahib, won't you join us for some tea?"

This anecdote is in Robert V. Levine's book *A Geography of Time*, and Altman describes it as follows:

> So I would have no choice but to sit down, and wait while some servant ran out to get me tea. Then Mr. Kahn would inquire about my wife, etc., and all the assembled people would have a million questions about my life, America, etc., etc., etc. It would be hard to know how to ask for my tomato seeds again. Eventually, after an hour or two, I would decide to risk being rude anyway. I would get my seeds and be on my way, noting that none of the people sitting around the desk had gotten their business taken care of.[4]

Levine finds that there are great differences around the world in the way people view time, and this has a profound effect on the social structures of a country. Until you learn to adjust to the local "clock speed," as it were, life can be quite annoying.

For an American, everything is hurry, hurry, hurry, so tasks get done on time. In America, lunch can be delayed or even skipped to finish a project, and airlines brag about their on-time performance. By contrast, a country where breaks are sacrosanct and *on time* is a relative term can take some getting used to for an American Peace Corps volunteer. Levine found this out for himself when he visited India as well.

He had gone to the train station in New Delhi, because that was the only place in the city to buy a ticket for the train he was hoping to catch later in the week. He really needed to take that train, and he really needed to get his ticket as soon as possible. He joined a long line of potential travelers, all heading for a single ticket window. He inched forward, and after an hour he reached the window. He recounts,

> The cashier greeted me with the familiar *Namaste* and immediately flipped up a sign that said "Closed for Lunch" (in English, I might add). With my blood pressure headed for Kashmir, I turned around to gather support for my case. But all my compatriots were already sitting on the floor, with their blankets spread out, eating picnic lunches. "What can I do?" I asked a couple next to me. "You can join us for lunch," they answered.[5]

Levine and his students have gone around the world, measuring the speed at which life progresses. Some of the observations are qualitative, but a few are quite concrete. For example, Levine has come up with an estimate for what he calls "the pace of life" by looking at how accurate clocks in public places are, how long it takes for a letter to be delivered, and how fast people walk.

Levine's table shows the results of his assessment comparing thirty-one countries. The numbers in the columns represent the ranking on each of the variables measured. The "faster" countries were primarily European, whereas the "slower" countries tended to be closer to the equator. The United States was in the middle.

One consequence of living life at a slower pace is that the scheduled starting times for appointments aren't carved in stone. Levine talks about *hora Mexicana*—the unspoken but universally understood fact that in Mexico, a meeting scheduled for 11 a.m. is really expected to start at 11:15. Or maybe 11:30. Or perhaps noon.

Ranking of Pace of Life Variables

Country	Overall Pace of Life	Walking Speed	Postal Time	Clock Accuracy
Switzerland	1	3	2	1
Ireland	2	1	3	11
Germany	3	5	1	8
Japan	4	7	4	6
Italy	5	10	12	2
England	6	4	9	13
United States	16	6	23	20
Syria	27	29	28	27
El Salvador	28	22	16	31
Brazil	29	31	24	28
Indonesia	30	26	26	30
Mexico	31	17	31	26

Robert V. Levine, *A Geography of Time: On Tempo, Culture, and the Pace of Life* (New York: Basic Books, 1997).

Another country where life is on the slow side is Brazil. According to Levine, people in Brazil are prepared to delay starting a birthday party for 129 minutes while waiting for a tardy guest to arrive. Contrast that with an American child's birthday party. In this country, after two hours the hosts are glancing at the door hoping the parents will arrive soon to retrieve their offspring rather than expecting new guests to start arriving.

Although there are some obvious annoyances with nations that take it slow, countries that rigidly adhere to rules about time can be just as annoying. A country famous for its clocks, Switzerland is also known for its adherence to rules. America is not without rules, but the inflexibility of Swiss rules can prove too much for some people.

Take the case of Wendy and Sidney Harris. They really do live in Switzerland, but they asked that we change their personal details since their story might offend people in their new country of residence.

Wendy and her husband are both lawyers. They moved to Zurich so that Sidney could take a job at an international law firm. They've worked in countries all over the world and faced every kind of bureaucratic hurdle imaginable. Yet their experiences in Zurich have convinced them that despite Switzerland's gorgeous scenery, wonderful chocolate, and clean cities, the country is the most annoying place they've ever lived.

Sidney tells the story of trying to arrange for private piano lessons for his daughter. He found a teacher and went to his studio to schedule the classes. The teacher had space in his calendar for weekly lessons, but there was a problem. The teacher always started his lessons to coincide with the school year. Alas, it was now October, a month after school had begun. Sidney's daughter would have to wait another year to start learning to play the piano. "But these are private lessons, what difference does it make?" Sidney protested. The teacher shook his head, as if he were dealing with some sort of imbecile, and explained once again that lessons began in September, and it was now October. Ultimately, Sidney found a teacher born in nearby France who was a bit more flexible.

Wendy has had similar experiences—like the time she tried to get the tires changed on their car. She had an 8 a.m. appointment, but traffic delayed her arrival. She wrote Sidney the following note about her experience:

> Unbelievable, it takes me 35 min to get to the car
> dealership, so I get there at 8:15, and [dealer] says

they can't do it in an hour or even 2. He carefully explains to me that the 10:00 coffee break and the lunch hour are sacred, you can't even pick up a car during the lunch break. Now that I'm 15 min late I can return on Dec. 5 [a few days later] for the next available 8 a.m. appointment. So, they kindly handed me a bus pass and I'll have to hoof it back here between 1:15 and 6:00. This shit drives me insane. No way am I ever having tires put on again. We'll do it ourselves. I find this stuff annoying beyond belief. Sorry, there's nothing you can do, I just have to vent.

If there's a saving grace about the persnicketyness of the Swiss way of doing things, it's that at least in Switzerland the rules can be articulated, and in some cases, they are even explicitly codified. That's rarely the case for social norms.

Anthropologist Edward T. Hall has made a study of social norms, beginning in World War II, when he spent time in Europe and the Philippines, and later when he was involved in training people for foreign service. In his 1966 book *The Hidden Dimension*, Hall describes his theory of "proxemics."[6] As Levine argues for time, Hall argues that culture shapes our perception of physical space—and who belongs in it. In every culture, only the closest friends and associates are allowed into our intimate space. There's a different comfort boundary for people we deal with in a social setting and yet another for people we interact with in a public setting. People who cross those boundaries are annoying. Yet so, too, is figuring out where those boundaries are in an unfamiliar country.

"A very good example is that a lot of Middle Easterners like to stand closer to people than we do in our Western culture," says Phoebe Ellsworth. "So, if you're at a party with someone who has a different sense of what the right distance to stand away is when you're talking to somebody, and he is too close, he can seem to us overbearing."

The consequences of these space violations can be amusing. "You frequently see an American take a step back," says Ellsworth, "and the Middle Easterner will take a step forward so he can get closer to his comfortable distance. They go around and around the room like that." It's like a dance.

In public places, where the interaction is not as close and personal, the need for space still exists. Elliot Aronson is a social psychologist at the University of California, Santa Cruz. He says that Greeks and Americans have very different ideas about how to distribute themselves on an empty stretch of beach. "On an American beach," says Aronson, "three people arrive and sit as far away from one another as they can. As more people arrive, they fill in, leaving space between strangers. On a Greek beach, three people arrive and immediately sit close together. You can see how Americans would be annoyed by a family of Greeks setting their towels down right next to them with 'room' available!"

There are also very different norms about whether you should look people in the eye, according to Ellsworth. "We think that it's the right thing to do," she says. "We take it as a sign of sincerity; we assume that if somebody is not looking us in the eye, maybe the person is lying. Yet many other cultures think it's rude to look somebody right in the eye."

She has observed this with many of her foreign students at the University of Michigan. Some of them have described to her the experience of driving a car and having their passengers try to make eye contact with them. She says they find it not only annoying but downright scary.

Ellsworth says that significant consequences can result from this cultural misunderstanding. A foreign visitor's discomfort with making eye contact with an immigration official or a security officer could arouse suspicion in an official who is untrained in these cultural norms.

Ellsworth has been trying to find out when these patterns of behavior emerge. She has begun a comparative analysis of American and Japanese children's books. As you might expect, the American books tell stories of individuals triumphing over adversity, whereas Japanese stories are more about fitting in and getting along. Ellsworth doubts that these patterns of behavior are something we're born with—she thinks it must be the result of early childhood experiences.

So, if we Americans as a culture have a narcissistic, self-assured swagger as we strut through the world, and if we are annoyed when our will is thwarted and events we can't control drive us nuts, we come by these attitudes honestly. Like so many of life's woes (and joys), it's all our parents' fault.

12

When Your Mind Becomes a Foreign Country

Chris Furbee spent most of his childhood in Philippi, a town on the banks of the Tygart River in central West Virginia. After Chris's parents got divorced, his mother couldn't afford their house in nearby Lake Floyd, so Chris and his mom moved into his grandparents' trailer in Philippi.

Quarters were tight. Chris remembers slinking past his grandfather as the old man lurched down the narrow hallways. "He'd lose balance and bump into me occasionally," Chris says. "I had a real hard time with it. I hate

to say that, but I was a teenager. I felt like it was almost
like he had a contagious disease." Chris's grandfather did
have a disease, but it wasn't contagious: he was dying of
Huntington's disease (HD).

The lurching is a symptom of the illness, caused by the
degeneration of the brain, particularly the basal ganglia,
which plays a role in motor function. The movement tics are
called *chorea*, the Greek word for "dance," but it looks more
like a marionette show. Imagine an invisible hand rhythmi-
cally pulling your limbs, your head, and even your tongue in
different directions. That's chorea. The tics are involuntary.
They don't hurt—until the end of the day, when your muscles
ache from the constant motion.

Losing control of your muscles is only one symptom of
Huntington's disease. You also slowly lose your mind: HD
patients have difficulty recollecting words, reading emotions
in others, learning new things, and remembering old information. Yet these symptoms appear later. Early on—even before
the chorea—researchers have found that the symptoms are
often more subtle personality changes. One hallmark of the
early disease is a feeling of being uncontrollably annoyed.

Although the symptom is defined as irritability, there is no
standard clinical definition of the term. Irritability has been
largely neglected by psychiatry, according to neuropsychia-
trist David Craufurd of the University of Manchester School
of Medicine in the United Kingdom. It's not particularly well
studied, well measured, or even well defined. Although irritability is a symptom of other mental illnesses—Tourette's
syndrome, autism, and personality disorders—Huntington's
disease is one of the few illnesses in which the behavior has
been systematically studied.

Understanding the brain changes that occur in Huntington's patients may reveal something about what triggers people to become annoyed and why some people are more prone than others to be irritable.

For healthy people, irritability could be thought of as a person's propensity to get annoyed. Craufurd, who has thought about irritability in Huntington's patients perhaps as much as anyone, says, "In common parlance in England, we say that somebody has a short fuse. Irritability is the length of your fuse, so to speak."

Another way to think about a short fuse, says Kevin Craig, a psychiatrist based in Cambridge, United Kingdom, is as a lens or a mood. Craig distinguishes emotions from moods. "The idea is that emotions have an object. So, if you're annoyed or surprised or disgusted, it's always at something or about something that's external to yourself." Surprise, happiness, and anger are emotions. The feeling of being annoyed might fit into the emotion category— it's often short-lived and prompted by something external. "Whereas with moods, it's more like a lens or a filter," Craig says.

For psychiatrists who treat Huntington's patients, it's not so much the irritable filter that's the problem, it's the expression of the irritability. "As psychiatrists, we don't deal as much in Huntington's with the internal state as we do with the external," says Karen Anderson, who runs the Huntington's clinic at the University of Maryland. It's not the *patients* who complain of feeling annoyed, Anderson says. "It's the family that sees the external manifestation."

HD patients with this symptom punch walls and damage property, kick over their children's bikes, and throw plates at their spouses because dinner was too salty. This is annoyance to the point of dysfunction. This is annoyance as a disease.

Chris Furbee remembers being aware of his mother's symptoms when he was thirteen and she was in her late thirties. She had movement tics—a subtler version of his grandfather's swaying. Huntington's symptoms usually start to appear at this age—around forty. He also remembers his mother acting annoyed: "This is all in hindsight. She seemed to be angry a lot. Back then, I just thought it was my mom being mean. But I think what happened was the disease affected her to the point where she was very irritable."

Yet Chris says it's hard to separate the disease from the circumstances. "A lot of that could have been the fact that she was living with her own parents, in this trailer in Philippi, West Virginia—it's not ideally where she wanted to be," he says. This is one of the difficulties with measuring irritability as a symptom of a disease. The details of your life make a difference. "It's easy not to be very irritable if you live in an environment where people don't impinge on you too much," says David Craufurd. "Somebody who lives alone, on the whole, tends to be less irritable than somebody who lives with teenage children, shall we say."

Chris left his mother when he was a teenager. At eighteen, he relocated to the San Francisco Bay area. His grandfather had died. His mom was still driving, showing only mild symptoms, he remembers. He went back a few times, and then years passed without a visit.

• • •

Huntington's is an inherited disease. Your likelihood of having it is written on the short arm of chromosome four. If one of your parents has the disease, you have a 50 percent chance of inheriting it. If you do not inherit the disease, you cannot pass it on—Huntington's in your family ends with you.

The gene that causes the disease, technically called IT15, holds the instructions for making the huntingtin protein. What, exactly, the protein does is still a mystery, but it appears to play an important role in nerve cell function. The disease occurs when instructions for the protein are screwed up. Specifically, the gene carrying the instructions includes a sequence of repeating base pairs—cyotosine-adenine-guanine (CAG). Ten to thirty-five CAG repeats on that gene is normal. Thirty-six to thirty-nine puts one at risk for developing the disease. Forty or more repeats, and you will get Huntington's, with no ambiguity in the prognosis. There is no cure or approved treatment for slowing the disease. Most people die fifteen to twenty years after they start to show symptoms.

The problem with the repeats in the instructions is that they cause the huntingtin protein to be built wrong. "It spoils the shape of the protein, and this has a functional effect of some sort," says Craufurd. If the language sounds vague, that's because our understanding of how that malformed protein wreaks havoc on the body and the brain isn't clear. "There are twenty-five different theories about what the problem is," says Karen Anderson, "but there is no good solid answer as to what is really going on, which is why we've had so much trouble targeting it with the treatment trials."

Although the mechanism isn't obvious, the effects are: the busted protein somehow causes muscles to waste away. The liver and the spleen suffer, Craufurd says. HD patients burn calories at a rapid rate, "which sounds wonderful until you realize they also have swallowing problems," says Anderson. "They can't possibly eat what most of us eat in a day, let alone enough food to burn four thousand calories in a day, which some of them easily can."

The brain, however, is the main target of the illness. It shrinks. Brain cells die, and the brain atrophies. One area that suffers the most is the basal ganglia—particularly, the caudate, a primitive section buried deep within the brain. The cerebral cortex also thins out, Craufurd says. "It's really quite widespread. It's not uniform throughout the brain. There are some areas where there's more atrophy than others. You can see that cortical atrophy starts quite early."

Like a domino effect, when one area of the brain dies, the connections from that area to other places die as well. Karen Anderson says, "As a result of the caudate dying, all of these connections to the frontal lobe and other parts of the brain also die off."

Brain-imaging techniques such as PET (positron emission tomography) scans and fMRI (functional magnetic resonance imaging) are helping researchers unravel just how the brain deteriorates. If the progression of the disease in the brain could be understood, it's possible that a symptom like irritability could be tied to particular brain circuitry. At this point, researchers are far from being able to make those connections. "I think that in ten years, we might have a really good answer to that question," says Karen Anderson. "Right now, we don't know enough about the progression of brain changes in Huntington's to be able to answer that." Anderson says it's likely that different patients will exhibit different patterns of cell death. "My thought is that there are some groups where the frontal cortex—the areas that control motivation—die out more. In others, there's circuitry that affects irritability, and those may die out more."

This is consistent with how the disease manifests. HD affects different people in different ways. Not all patients are irritable. Chris's grandfather, for example, didn't seem to show signs of irritability.

Chris went back to West Virginia when he was twenty-eight. When he walked into the house, "it looked like a tornado had hit," he says. Food-encrusted plates and cups of milk that had been sitting out for days littered the counters. Cigarette burns pocked the carpet. A woman was lying limply on the couch. Her cheeks were sunken. Her hair was a mess. Her body was skeletal. She wasn't moving. Chris wasn't sure whether she was breathing. He walked into the kitchen to look for his mother. When he walked back into the living room, the woman on the couch opened her eyes and smiled at him. He left the house and broke down.

Chris also brought a video camera on this trip. He had the idea to do a documentary on Huntington's disease, although, he says, "I had no idea what I was going to shoot, until I got there." Chris couldn't bring himself to film the house when he first got home. He regrets that. He did set up a "makeshift studio in one part of the garage" and used it to do self-interviews. He shot twenty hours of footage in the two months that he stayed with his mom. During the last fifteen years, he has relived that period of his life again and again while editing the tape. As you might suspect, he says, "It is painful to watch that footage over and over."

Chris's mom, despite the severe chorea, refused to admit that she had the disease. She had told Chris that if she ever started to show signs of the illness, she would kill herself. So Chris never got to talk to his mom about the disease. The denial also complicated the filming—"I couldn't just say to her, 'Hey, Mom, I'm doing a documentary on Huntington's disease,' because she never admitted that she had it, and any time I would bring up Huntington's disease, she would start talking about suicide. That was a conversation I never wanted to have with my mom."

A year after that visit, when Chris was twenty-nine, he decided to get tested for Huntington's. "I just felt like I needed to know what direction to go in my life. I felt like I was stuck. I felt like the best thing to do was to find out if I had inherited the gene. I'm working on this documentary, and I'm about ready to find out my test results. I thought, 'I hope I get some good news, but it would be great for the film if I got bad news.'" It was bad news.

Now, at age forty-three, Chris is showing mild chorea and says he's a little more forgetful and words are harder to retrieve. His documentary is almost entirely shot, and he's holding annual fund-raisers to bankroll the production of the rest of it. He makes regular speaking appearances to educate people about Huntington's. For the last nine years, he's been working with mentally ill adults—mainly, schizophrenics—who live in something like an assisted-living home, only it is for people with mental illness. The residents can come and go as they please, but there are always caretakers like Chris around. Chris says that he would like to see the same model of care for people with Huntington's disease.

Care of HD patients is a challenge that often falls on family members, until the burden becomes too much. One of the main reasons people with Huntington's are put into nursing homes, according to some studies, is irritability.

Psychiatrists such as Karen Anderson say that they spend a lot of time educating the families of HD patients. "A lot of it is teaching people that this loved one or this patient who used to be a reasonable person five or ten years ago is not the same," Anderson says. "You can't reason things out anymore because that part of the brain is not working the way it should."

Although the symptoms can't be traced to exact circuits, general brain regions are implicated in regulating irritability. Psychiatrist Jon Silver points to the frontal lobes. "Data have shown that irritability and aggression are correlated with frontal lobe lesions," Silver says.

Silver specializes in treating patients with traumatic brain injury (TBI). The most commonly injured parts of the brain are the frontal and temporal lobes (mostly due to car accidents and falls)—which means there is some overlap between the brain areas affected in TBI patients and Huntington's patients.

Irritability in Huntington's patients and TBI patients manifests in a similar way: a short fuse that ends in a giant explosion. This is how Silver describes it: "If you're crossing the street in Manhattan, and a car comes close to you as a pedestrian, what do you do? What do you do to the driver or the car? You don't scream at him, you don't hit the car. Right? My patients do."

Your frontal lobes are thought to be the brakes for your most basic wants. Think of the frontal lobes as the gatekeeper for your limbic system. The limbic system—which includes the hippocampus, the amygdala, the anterior thalamic nuclei, and the limbic cortex—is your primal urge center. Do you feel hungry? It's your limbic system telling you. Do you want to have sex? It's your limbic system knocking. The idea is that without your frontal lobes to regulate your desires, you'd simply do these things without worrying about the consequences.

When you have a disease that affects your frontal lobes, Silver says, "You can't inhibit your responses and deal with the stressors as well as you can when your frontal lobes are working well. What we're saying is that the frontal lobe is in charge of inhibiting the limbic system." Although many areas of the brain can play a role in anger and aggression, Silver believes that the frontal lobes play perhaps the most important role in regulating irritability.

If true, this suggests that getting annoyed over minor provocations is an inhibition problem. In other words, we all have this capacity for extreme responses, but most of us have frontal lobes that tamp down the annoyed reaction. Mark Groves puts it simply: "Our frontal lobes help inhibit inappropriate responses or impulsive responses. And our patients who have damage to these circuits lose their ability to inhibit those behaviors."

Irritability is one of the earliest symptoms of Huntington's, according to a study conducted by David Craufurd.[1] He found that HD patients were irritable five to ten years before motor symptoms appeared. As the HD progresses and more of the brain dies, however, irritability is overcome by indifference. Groves says, "One symptom that you see in basal ganglia disease is apathy. The more damage, the more apathy in Parkinson's and Huntington's." One interpretation is that the basal ganglia—which is primarily associated with motor function—also helps us decide between different actions. In any given moment we're faced with a huge array of behavioral choices, and it's thought that this region of the brain helps you select the best one. When it's not functioning, decisions are harder to make. Your brain can't choose, so it chooses nothing.

One interesting symptom of Huntington's that may shine light on the nature of irritability is that HD patients are apt to misconstrue situations, researchers say. Craufurd was the coauthor of a study that tested the ability of Huntington's patients to read social cues by asking the participants to interpret cartoons. Identifying the humor in the cartoons required the viewer to infer the mental state of another person. Here's the description from the paper in *Neuropsychologia*:

> In one cartoon, for example, a man is shown cuddling a young woman who is sitting on his lap, while with his free hand, he is tapping a ping-pong ball with a bat. The humor lies in the fact that an older woman sitting in the adjacent room, within earshot but out of view of the couple, is deceived into believing that the man is playing table tennis, whereas in reality he is otherwise occupied.[2]

Huntington's patients were asked to describe why the cartoon was funny. Here's a misread that one HD patient made: "They're having a bit of nooky while the wife's sat [*sic*] in there. She's thinking, 'At least, he's leaving me alone. Peace!'"

The interpretation isn't like the paranoid delusion of a schizophrenic; it's within the realm of possible reality, but it is not supported by the information presented. The authors of the study write, "HD patients did draw inferences that went beyond the physical contents of the cartoon. They abstracted and formulated hypotheses, including hypotheses about a character's feelings or belief. However, those inferences deviated from the conventional interpretation."

This tendency to misconstrue seems to exacerbate the irritability problem. We have all met someone who takes things the wrong way. Let's say you tell your husband that his suit makes him look trim, and he responds, "Are you saying I'm fat?" People who are prone to reading too much into a statement or a situation also seem prone to getting annoyed. Kevin Craig said that many of his depressed patients are irritable, and it seems to be related to their tendency to assume the worst, even if there's no evidence for the assumption. "They take things the wrong way," he says. "Neutral comments become upsetting." In the case of Huntington's patients, the combination of being likely to misconstrue and having a short fuse because your mental brakes aren't working well can result in disaster.

Breaking a social contract is a common source of annoyance, even for healthy people. Most of us navigate the world with expectations for how social situations should transpire, and we get annoyed when those expectations are not fulfilled: a quiet train ride is disrupted by a noisy nail-clipper, a simple meeting in India becomes a lengthy afternoon tea, or a Swiss mechanic won't honor your appointment because you're a little late. Now imagine that social transactions never go the way you expect. It's like waking up in a foreign country where all of the rules are different, and you're never able to decode them. Craufurd gives this example:

> I like to tell a story of my patient who was actually on his way to the clinic. He comes from Liverpool, and he leaves his bag in the gent's toilet in the railway station. The person who saw him do this approached a policeman who then eventually found [the patient] and reunited him with his bag and gave him a rather annoying lecture about being more careful in the future. [The patient] ended up hitting this policeman and getting arrested. One part of it is obviously being able to think through the consequences of actions, and you'd know that hitting a policeman would get you into big trouble. But aside from that, you and I wouldn't regard that person as threatening, he's just doing his job, and if you couldn't really correctly infer that, you might think that he was angry and that he represented some kind of physical threat.

Compounding the problem for Huntington's patients is that according to one of Craufurd's studies, people with the disease are particularly bad at recognizing negative emotions, especially anger, in others.[3] Most healthy people can look at someone's furrowed brow or other facial features and recognize anger or sadness. Huntington's patients have a particularly hard time with this. "Patients with Huntington's aren't terrifically good at correctly reading another person's emotional state, and that leaves you at a great disadvantage," Craufurd says.

This is a social impediment because the reactions of others often direct our own behavior. Imagine how you might behave if you didn't know you were making others feel bad. You might act much worse if you didn't see the negative consequences to others.

For a healthy person, making your spouse upset (and having to deal with that upsetness) might deter you from making a big fuss over a trivial matter. If you couldn't see that your spouse was upset—because your brain wasn't functioning properly—you might not feel quite as deterred. An incentive for regulating our tendency to get annoyed may have something to do with guilt avoidance. So, it's a triple threat for some Huntington's patients: the disease can make a person more likely to misread a situation, make it difficult for a person to control himself, and impair his ability to recognize that his behavior is making someone sad or angry.

Worse still, HD patients don't seem to be particularly aware of their outbursts, psychiatrists say. Mark Groves relates this story from the Huntington's clinic at Columbia University: "This morning in the clinic there was one patient we saw recently. I asked her, 'Have you been irritable lately?' and she said, 'No.' Then her husband said, 'Yes, you have been.' And she screamed out, '¡Mentira!' [It's a lie!] and started to lunge at him—of course, demonstrating that she was irritable."

Because the patients are unreliable sources, David Craufurd is interested in figuring out whether irritability can be measured directly. "We started to play around a little bit with experimental paradigms to try to annoy people and see whether we could measure a response to that." Specifically, Craufurd and colleagues, including Stefan Klöppel, put healthy people and people with the Huntington's gene into an fMRI machine and annoyed them.[4]

The participants were playing a game—but the researchers were cheating them. "The results were a little bit confusing from that study," Craufurd says. In the healthy participants, "when we cheated them with the computer, their imaging showed the brain changes we rather expected when people start to get annoyed." The researchers saw activation of the amygdala—which is part of the limbic system—when the healthy participants reported feeling annoyed. "Whereas the [HD] patients showed the same sort of brain changes when they were provoked, but they said they didn't feel annoyed, and that rather spoiled the correlations and so on," Craufurd says. Even though their brain activity suggested annoyance, patients with HD weren't aware of the feeling or didn't admit to feeling annoyed.

The good news for HD patients—and perhaps even better news for their families and caretakers—is that irritability can be treated. "It's remarkably responsive to treatment, so it's very gratifying," says Mark Groves, who is working on treatment guidelines for HD.

The first line of attack for irritability is drugs. When treating irritability, Groves says, "more than in any other area of psychiatry, I am confident when I give a prescription to our patients in the HD clinic that either a family member is going to call or the patient is going to call and say this is tremendously helpful."

Four classes of medication are used to treat irritability. Groves likes to start with selective serotonin reuptake inhibitors (SSRIs)—a group that includes antidepressants such as Lexapro, Celexa, Prozac, and Zoloft. Serotonin is a neurotransmitter that helps deliver messages in the brain. SSRIs block the absorption of serotonin by certain nerve cells in the brain, leaving more serotonin floating around. If some circuits are down, as occurs in HD patients, it seems to help to make the nerve cells that are working more effective.

Groves says that unlike with depression, in HD this irritability disappears within a few weeks on these medications. "Irritability in Huntington's seems cleaner. It's extreme, but it also melts away on the medications. Whereas the irritability in some of the other conditions, it's more complex, especially for personality disorders or depression or bipolar disorder." Psychiatrist Jon Silver has seen irritability evaporate in only few days in his traumatic brain injury patients.

There are other medications that Groves uses as well, such as propranolol, a beta-blocker, which is often prescribed as a blood pressure medication. "People use propranolol all of the time for performance anxiety. It prevents the adrenaline or norepinephrine surge that causes your blood pressure to go up, your heart rate to go up. So it's very interesting that this would work. It's not an antidepressant at all."

Dopamine-blocking medications that are approved for autism are also sometimes used. And mood stabilizers—antiepileptic or antiseizure medications—are used as well, Groves says.

In addition to drugs, the other treatment for irritability is getting rid of annoyances. This seems relevant to anyone who suffers from irritability, not only to those with a disease. Here are some tips from the psychiatrists: skipping meals makes most people, healthy or ill, more irritable. Mark Groves says that he eats an energy bar before he goes home, so that he's not irritable when he arrives. Sleep deprivation is another irritability inducer.

People are also more likely to become annoyed when they are faced with unforeseen situations, Karen Anderson says. We don't do well with surprises, and that's especially true for HD patients. "A lot of what we do with patients and families is making sure things are very structured. You prepare people ahead of time if there's going to be a doctor's visit or a visit from a family member they haven't seen in a long time. A lot of it is scheduling and minimizing surprises. That's something that I think can help anyone cut down on irritability on a day-to-day basis."

Huntington's patients indicate what happens to annoyance when the brain breaks down, but what accounts for annoyance in healthy brains?

13

The Annoyed Brain

It was 10:53 on a Tuesday morning, and Patti wasn't going to make it to the lab on time. She'd stayed up late the night before and then slept through the alarm. The year was 2006, and Patti was a sophomore at the University of Southern California. It wouldn't be unfair to call Patti a typical college sophomore. She wasn't a star student, but she managed a B+ average, spiking the occasional A in English because she was a pretty good writer.

She hadn't decided on a major but was leaning toward psychology. That's why she'd signed up to be a subject in the psych experiment she was running late for. She was supposed to be at the cognitive neuroimaging center over by the Seely-Mudd building at eleven to have her brain scanned.

Tom Denson, a graduate psych student, was running the experiment. Denson led one of the sections in Patti's intro psych class. She saw an ad he had placed on the department's Web site looking for participants in a study he was doing on cognitive ability and mental imagery.

Two weeks earlier, she had been to Denson's office to answer a long set of questions. It was the kind of personality stuff she recognized from the intro psych course: Do you get along with others? Do you like to show off? Do other people misunderstand you? Do you worry about what people think of you? "He just wants to know how neurotic I am," Patti thought.

Some of the agree-disagree items were a little more unexpected: I get into fights more than the average person. Sometimes I fly off the handle for no good cause. When things don't go the way I plan, I take out my frustration on the first person I see. If I have had a hard day at work or school, I'm likely to make sure everyone knows about it. "What's he getting at there?" she wondered at the time.

On this morning, however, she wasn't thinking about those questions. All she was thinking about was getting to the imaging center by eleven, and she wasn't going to make it. At ten past eleven, she blew in the front door and went to the room where Denson had told her to meet him. He was a thinnish, gangly man with glasses. He didn't seem annoyed that she was late, but he was anxious to get started. He handed her a clipboard. On the clipboard was a list of words. Next to each word were the numbers 1 to 5. "Before we do the scanning stuff, I want to see how you're feeling today. Rate your feelings on each of these words, where 1 is 'not at all' and 5 is 'extremely.'"

There were about sixty-five words on the list, adjectives such as *alert, angry, considerate, shaky,* and *sad.* It took her about two minutes to jot down her ratings. "Right, let's head over to the lab," said Denson.

The lab was in the adjacent room. From the control room, Patti could see the magnetic resonance imaging machine through the open door. It resembled a huge, thick white donut. Sticking out of the hole in the center of the donut was a thin platform, like the gangplank into a ship.

Patti knew the basics of how an MRI worked. The device contained a huge, powerful magnet that produced a strong electromagnetic field. When the magnet was pulsed on and off, it caused the protons in water molecules to change their orientation, a change that the device could detect. By adjusting the orientation of the magnetic field, computers could build a three-dimensional picture of the tissue structure of whatever was in the scanner. Today, that tissue would be Patti's brain.

She'd looked at the safety material Denson had sent her. She knew there was no health risk from getting the scan. The only real risk was if she got near the magnet with anything metal in her pockets or, even worse, anything metal inside her—say, a metal pin to hold a broken bone together. The magnet could rip that pin out of her body.

She remembered one caution that amused her: "It is a good idea not to wear eye makeup—tiny metal bits in mascara, for example, can move in the magnetic field and irritate your eyes."[1] "One advantage of being late," she thought. "No time for makeup this morning."

"Here's the drill," Denson told her. "You'll lie down in the machine. You'll have on a pair of headphones. Try to keep your head as still as possible. You'll be able to see a small screen above your head. Jumbled-up letters will appear on the screen. Your job is to tell me what word the letters spell when you put them in the right order."

"So you want me to solve the anagrams?" she asked.

"Exactly," said Denson. "There's a microphone inside the MRI. I'll be able to hear your answers. You have fifteen seconds to solve each anagram. If you don't know the answer, just say 'No answer.' Clear?"

"Clear."

"But before we start showing you the anagrams, we'll take a baseline scan. All you have to do is lie there."

"I think I can handle that," Patti said.

"Then let's get started."

She put on the headphones and lay down on the gangplank. Her head was resting in a plastic cage with foam sides that helped keep her head from moving. Denson left the room and the gangplank retracted into the machine. It stopped when Patti's entire torso was inside the machine, with only her legs sticking out.

"Can you hear me?" Denson asked.

"Loud and clear," she replied.

"Good," he said, "and I can hear you, too. So, here we go with the baseline run. Just lie still."

The silence that had engulfed her inside the machine was replaced by a whirring sound and then intermittent banging. The banging came on again and stayed on.

"What's that sound?" Patti asked.

"It's the sound the machine makes when it's running," said Denson. "Sorry, there's nothing we can do about that. Just lie quietly while we take a baseline measurement."

She lay still, thinking that the banging would become annoying after a while. After five or six minutes, she heard Denson's voice in her ear again. "Now we're ready to start the experiment. Here come the anagrams. Remember, you'll have fifteen seconds to solve each one. You'll hear a beep when the time is up. Either say what the unscrambled word is or say, 'No answer.' Be sure to speak in a loud voice so I can hear you. I'll record your answers here in the control room. Here we go."

The screen went dark, and then the letters "zapzi" appeared on the screen. "Pizza," Patti said after a few seconds.

The next anagram appeared: sems. This one took a little longer, but Patti got it before the beep. "Mess," she said.

"You'll have to speak up, I can't hear you," she heard Denson say over her headphones.

"Mess," she repeated more loudly.

The next couple of anagrams were pretty easy. Then came "auletenitn." Patti stared at the letters. She mentally flipped them around, but nothing was coming. The beep sounded. "No answer," she said.

"I thought I told you to speak up," she heard Denson say.

"No answer!" she said again, this time practically shouting. "Can't they get their own equipment to work?" she fumed to herself.

The letters "neentroivmn" appeared on the screen. "Cripes, I have no idea," she thought. "I wish that banging would stop." The beep sounded again.

"No answer," she said loudly.

"Speak up," Denson said in her ear. "Look, this is the third time I have had to say this!" He sounded pissed off. "Can't you follow directions?"

"This totally sucks," Patti thought. "How am I supposed to answer questions in this environment? And why the heck can't he hear me? He's either deaf, or this equipment isn't working. And why am I not seeing any more words?"

"I'm cutting short the experiment," Denson said after a minute or two had passed. "Before we end, I'm going to project a series of statements on the screen. You don't have to do anything. Just read the statements and think about them." He added sarcastically, "Do you think you can do that?"

Patti didn't say anything, because she was pretty sure Denson wouldn't want to hear what she really wanted to say to him.

The first statement flashed on the screen: "Think about whom you have interacted with in the experiment up to this point." About a dozen similar statements followed. Finally, Denson's voice came back into her ears. "We're finished now."

"And not a moment too soon," thought Patti. "That was totally annoying. I'm never going to sign up for another experiment. Maybe I should change majors."

The previous story is essentially true, although some of the details were changed, and Patti is a hypothetical composite of the twenty students who participated in the experiment. Thomas Denson is extremely real.

As you may have suspected, this wasn't an experiment about cognition at all. Basically, a scientist put an unsuspecting subject into a brain scanner and annoyed her to see what happens in her brain. Denson was technically studying anger, but he's willing to concede the point. "As far as I know, no one has really argued for annoyance as a separate, discrete emotion from anger," he says. "I would say annoyance is the low level of anger, with rage being on the extreme end."

Because he has to convince review committees that his research is ethical before he is allowed to carry it out, he admits that he really is only trying to annoy people in his experiments. "We're not really allowed to make people excessively angry," says Denson. "But we wanted to do something realistic. Everyone's had a boss who said, 'Look, you really screwed this up.' And that makes you feel stupid. People tend to respond with annoyance to that."

After the subjects came out of the MRI, they completed something called the Positive and Negative Affect Schedule. It's a scale that measures how angry/annoyed someone is. Only after the subjects filled out this final questionnaire did Denson tell them what the experiment was really about. There are no published data on whether they were in a forgiving mood after the experiment was over. Denson says there were several factors designed to get the subjects annoyed. First, the anagrams: "A couple of the anagrams were easy. But most were really hard. Words like 'lieutenant' and 'environment.' Words with lots of vowels. And because we told them this was a test of their cognitive ability," in other words, how smart they were, "they were really invested in it. They wanted to do well."

Of course, they didn't do well, and that alone got the subjects annoyed. Then there was the banging of the MRI. That was a freebie. All MRIs make a version of that annoying banging. "The key part is that at three different points I interrupted them," says Denson.

The first two times he spoke in a calm voice, asking the subjects to speak up, even though he could hear them perfectly well. The third time, however, Denson tried to sound like he was losing his cool and getting pissed off. "That was all part of the script," says Denson.

When the subjects were good and annoyed, Denson took another brain image. Denson used a special form of MRI called functional MRI. Instead of using the machine to map structures in the brain, an fMRI measures where blood is flowing in the brain. The more brain cells are active in a particular region, the more blood flows to that region, suggesting that this particular area is implicated in whatever behavior or emotion a researcher is measuring.

In this case Denson measured which brain areas were active when the subjects were lying quietly inside the MRI and compared that with where the blood flowed when they were annoyed. What he found was that an area called the dorsal anterior cingulate cortex was most active at the end of the experiment when his subjects were all riled up. This is a part of the limbic system. The limbic system is in the forebrain. It's a system of brain regions that seems to be more involved with emotion than with rational thought. In Huntington's and traumatic brain injury patients, the theory is that their irritability is linked to the inability to regulate their limbic systems because of damage to their frontal lobes.

Denson says that the dorsal anterior cingulate cortex is "a pretty interesting little region, because it's sort of like the gatekeeper between automatic or unconscious processes and more conscious processes." Denson agrees with many psychologists who believe that most people go through their days in automatic mode, more or less on autopilot. Consider the experience of driving home from work. You've done it a million times. It's totally routine. You get home, and you suddenly think, "Whoa, what just happened?" You have no specific recollection of the drive home.

Some psychologists call this "autopilot" the x-system. It's not that you are unconscious as you go through your day, it's simply that you are not at that heightened level of attention that you would be if you were trying to find your way around in an unfamiliar city. Autopilot doesn't work in that circumstance, because nothing is routine. You have to pay close attention to everything, or you'll get lost.

Denson says that the dorsal anterior cingulate cortex switches you from autopilot mode into active attention mode. "So, take the same example," he says. "You're driving home, and now suddenly someone cuts you off and then flips you off for good measure. That dorsal anterior cingulate cortex is going to be active. It's going to wake up and say, 'Hey, I need some higher brain functions to come on board here and help me solve this problem.' So, it wakes the brain up."

This squares well with the explanation of annoyances being like halfalogues: they tend to be a disruption, and their unpredictability puts you in a heightened state of alertness. You can't tune them out.

Denson believes that's what happened in his experiment. The subjects came to the lab, like good college sophomores in psychology experiments are supposed to do. They expected to be treated in a certain way, and their minds were most likely focused entirely on other things. "And suddenly I'm treating them like kindergarteners. So the dorsal anterior cingulate cortex gets active."

Denson also wanted to see whether the subjects who were the angriest by the end of the experiment were also the ones who had the most blood flowing to the dorsal anterior

cingulate cortex. That's what the mood-and-aggression questionnaires were all about. Indeed, he did see a correlation
between the level of anger and blood flow to the dorsal anterior cingulate cortex, but this was a small study—only twenty
people—so sweeping conclusions are premature.

The limbic system's role in annoyance is probably a crucial
one. Brain responses in the limbic system are only somewhat
under our conscious control. You can learn that a particular
dark cave doesn't pose a danger, but you will always feel at
least a tingle of apprehension when you enter one. You can
learn to control your annoyance with someone or something,
but somewhere deep down, the limbic system will still insist
that the annoying wail of a baby's cry is something you want
to turn off if you possibly can.

The more "rational" part of the brain is usually associated with the cortex. The word *rational* is in quotes because
numerous authors have shown that people can be counted on
to behave irrationally. Maybe a better word is *cognitive*. It's
the part of the brain that considers the facts at hand, evaluates
them, and then makes some decision—rational or not—on
how to behave next. In Huntington's patients, this part of the
brain deteriorates, which may partly explain the emotional
outbursts.

One way to find out the role of a particular part of the
brain structure is to see how people behave without it.
Occasionally, this happens: parts are essentially "removed"
because of a stroke or some other brain injury. There are also
many cases where brain areas are removed as a procedure in
a medical therapy. Some neurosurgeons have removed part

of a patient's anterior cingulate cortex in order to treat psychiatric disorders such as major depression, schizophrenia, aggression, anxiety, and substance abuse. Cingulotomy, as it is technically known, has also been used on patients with chronic pain.

"Cingulotomy evolved as a better solution than frontal lobotomy," says neuroscientist Ron Cohen of Brown University. "The idea was that rather than do the whole removal of the frontal cortex"—a procedure that brought about a rainbow of psychological changes—surgeons "would try to get this area that was more specifically tied into the emotional systems and pain systems and things like that."

Most of the studies on patients who have undergone cingulotomy focus on whether their main symptoms were relieved. Cohen conducted one, however, that actually looked at the changes in emotional states in patients who elected to have the surgery.[2] The patients in this study were being treated for intractable pain. After the surgery, researchers gave them standard personality questionnaires and mood-measurement tools like the ones Denson used with his subjects.

Most of the patients did get relief from their pain following surgery, according to the authors. None experienced severe negative emotional side effects from their surgery. Yet there did appear to be personality changes. The families of many of the patients reported that after surgery, the patients tended to be perceived as being more relaxed or laid back. "In some cases," the authors wrote, "These changes were described as mild apathy and a lack of initiative after surgery." The patients themselves tended not to be aware of major personality changes, other than reporting less emotional tension, anger, and pain.

Howard Wilkinson performed the surgeries on the patients in Cohen's study. He is a neurosurgeon at Massachusetts General Hospital in Boston. Wilkinson has performed numerous cingulotomies, mostly to control chronic pain. He says patients who have the surgery still feel pain, it simply doesn't bother them as much. "A constant, chronic, ongoing irritation or pain fades away," says Wilkinson, "and people are less annoyed by the pain."

Wilkinson's study didn't look specifically at whether postoperative patients were less likely to be annoyed in general, "but they did seem calmer," he says. "The emotional state seemed slightly flatter."

This fits with Cohen's ideas of the role of the cingulate as a gateway to annoyance. All of the disorders that cingulotomy is used to treat involve what Cohen calls an "obsessive, ruminative loop." When the surgery works, Cohen says that it breaks the loop and allows people to live with, if not actually to ignore, the stimulus they are obsessing over, whether it's something unpleasant, such as pain or fingernails on a blackboard, or even when it's pleasant, like gambling or taking cocaine.

Of course, this "calmer" state makes it seem that it's not only annoyances that cingulotomy patients are less bothered by. Still, when neuroscientists trace the pathways of annoyance in the brain, as they are certain someday to do, it's likely that the anterior cingulate cortex will be an important part of the route.

Another way to get at how the brain processes annoyances is to look at patients with amnesia. Never mind the amnesia depicted in Hollywood movies, where the hero suddenly remembers he's a super spy. This is genuine amnesia, where people can form no new memories at all.

One of the best-studied cases of amnesia was a patient known only by the initials H.M. while he was alive. Henry Gustav Molaison died in 2008 at the age of eighty-two. When he was a child, he was hit by a bicycle. The accident caused him to start having severe seizures. When he was twenty-seven, surgeons removed a portion of his brain as a way to bring the seizures under control. The operation was a success, but it left Molaison with a very unusual problem. He couldn't form any new memories.

You could walk into a room where Molaison was sitting, introduce yourself to him, chat for a minute or two, leave the room, return a few minutes later, and he'd have no memory whatever of having met you. To make things even stranger, he remembered lots of details from his life before the surgery—just nothing new that happened.

It turns out that one portion of the surgical procedure involved removing a part of Molaison's brain known as the hippocampus, as well as some nearby related brain structures. It's a region that appears to be crucial for consolidating memory. It's not as if Molaison had no memory at all. He could hold a conversation, which meant remembering what someone had just said to him, but storing that memory, remembering the conversation for more than a minute or two, is impossible without a hippocampus and its neighboring brain regions.

Since scientists identified Molaison's problem, they have found many more patients with damage to this part of the brain who experience the same memory deficits. Yet the kinds of memories that are lost without a hippocampus are what psychologists call declarative memories, memories for things such as names, faces, facts, and figures. Declarative memories require a conscious, thinking brain.

There are other kinds of memories that don't require this kind of conscious thought. Think of how you learned to ride a bicycle. You don't say to yourself, "Okay, step over the seat, hold onto the handlebars, put one foot on the pedal, push off, start peddling, don't fall over." No, you simply get on and ride. Remembering that a flame can burn you also does not use much of your conscious brain. Remembering that dark alleys can be dangerous places is more of an emotional memory. Even if you've never been attacked in a dark alley, a feeling of danger is associated with it.

So, what kind of memory is involved in remembering that someone or something was annoying? Although the definitive study has yet to be performed, neuroscientist Daniel Tranel of the University of Iowa thinks he knows the answer. Tranel works with a lot of amnesic patients. Consider, he says, the following scenario: "You are flying on a long-distance trip, say, three or four hours, and in the row ahead of you are a mother and her small baby. The baby begins to cry, on and off. At first, you are not much bothered, hoping that the crying will subside. But it doesn't subside and keeps up for the next two hours, with the baby crying out in a very annoying way every so often. This gets more and more annoying and prevents you from sleeping, working, and otherwise relaxing and enjoying your trip."

Now, Tranel asks, what would happen if you had severe damage to your hippocampus? "First, you would not remember the baby crying from one time to the next, because the time between cries is at least many minutes and beyond the time frame for which you can retain new declarative knowledge. You would, however, become annoyed. Despite not having any declarative memory of the baby or of the fact that the baby has cried before (many times), you would have built up an emotional response to this."

In other words, each time the baby cried, you would experience the emotion of annoyance, and that emotional response could persist and even strengthen to the point where you would be very annoyed. "In that respect, your response is like that of a normal person, that is, extreme annoyance. Unlike a normal person, however, you do not have any declarative memory of the cause of your annoyance." So you'd be annoyed, but you wouldn't know exactly why. "This prediction is based on some of our recent work with amnesic patients," says Tranel, "which has demonstrated that the patients *do* have persistent emotions, despite not having a declarative memory of what caused the emotion in the first place."

Larry Squire at the University of California, San Diego, agrees with Tranel's conclusions. Squire says the part of the brain that is essential for forming and retaining these emotional memories is the amygdala. The amygdala is another part of the limbic system, that portion of the forebrain that also contains the cingulate cortex.

So if the amygdala or some other part of the limbic system is damaged, does that mean, in Tranel's hypothetical scenario, that the airline passenger would remember that there was a crying baby on his flight but will not feel annoyed by its intermittent crying? Yes, says Squire. "We did that experiment a long time ago with monkeys." He removed a portion of a monkey's amygdala and then compared monkeys lacking amygdalas with those whose amygdalas were intact. "We tested them on various emotional reactivity, fearful stimuli. It was only the monkeys without the amygdalas that showed any abnormality on that test."

There's one other scenario to consider here. What if, in addition to missing your hippocampus, you're missing your cingulate cortex as well, and once again, let's say, you are sitting behind that annoying baby?

The missing hippocampus would prevent you from remembering the last time the baby cried, and the missing cingulate would presumably keep you from becoming annoyed each time you heard it. So, in this scenario, the plane ride with the squalling baby would be, if not bliss, at least no worse than any other plane ride in today's crowded skies.

14

False Alarms

Usually, it's fun to sit in the bleachers. Maybe it's the altitude, but there's something easygoing about the patrons up there—bleacher bums dress casually, bring snacks, and seem to have a pretty good time. That also goes for the upper decks of a Broadway theater.

It was a rainy fall evening in Manhattan. Jude Law was playing a particularly well-dressed and anguished Hamlet at the Broadhurst Theatre on Broadway. The views from the upper decks were good and not obstructed. By the time the prince saw ghostly visions of his father, a pack of cellophane-wrapped Twizzlers was being passed around the last row.

That's when the problem started. One patron wasn't amused. Every Twizzler extraction prompted her to whip her head around and shoot icy glares. Then two people nearby slid a box of Good&Plenty out of a backpack. Even the most gingerly shake of the carton produced a loud sigh from the woman. Yet it was the Goobers at stage right that sent the lady over the edge. Without sugarcoating it, she went nuts. "*Stop eating.*" It was a whisper-yell, accompanied by a little fist bang on the armrest—but it was loud enough so that heads turned, up and down the aisle.

It's possible that junk food is this woman's pet peeve—maybe she's a dentist or a personal trainer, and it qualifies as a "professional annoyance." Maybe there's some cognitive overlay that we could never guess. Or, perhaps a more depressing explanation is that this particular person suffers from a genetic predisposition to getting annoyed.

Sarina Rodrigues is a neuroscientist in the Psychology Department at Oregon State University. Her research points to one way in which genetics could play a role in irritability and what that could mean for treating annoyance. Rodrigues is broadly interested in how our brains process emotions, and her approach is to study oxytocin. It is a chemical that acts as both a neurotransmitter and a hormone and has been implicated in trust, generosity, romantic attachment, and sex. In prairie voles (*Microtus ochrogaster*), oxytocin has been shown to work sort of like Cupid's arrow. When oxytocin was injected into the brain of a female vole, she rapidly fell for the nearest he-vole around.[1]

Oxytocin is manufactured in the hypothalamus region of our brains; it acts locally to help brain cells communicate over short distances and travels far afield to places such as the uterus and the heart, where it acts as a hormone. Like all hormones, oxytocin doesn't do anything without a receptor. The receptor is a protein sticking out of the membranes of cells. When oxytocin wafts by, it engages with the receptor, which sets off a chemical cascade inside the cell. Like a car key, it doesn't do much on its own, but with a turn, it activates a lot of sophisticated machinery.

Not all cells have all receptors. This is partly why certain hormones have specific effects—because they can interact only with certain cells. And some cells have more receptors than others: in places where reactivity is crucial to keeping us alive, such as where nerves and muscles meet to control our movements, a muscle cell can have ten thousand receptors per square micron.

There are receptors for oxytocin in cells all over the body, from the heart to the nervous system. Oxytocin fits into only one specific receptor, Rodrigues says. It's as if oxytocin turns on only one make of car, which makes life simpler for the researchers studying it. The oxytocin receptor is coded by a gene on chromosome three. Rodrigues and her colleagues wanted to know whether a variation in this gene had any affect on a person's behavior—specifically, on a person's reaction to stress.

Oxytocin calms us down when we're stressed, Rodrigues says. "It plays a key role in attenuating how much our emotional centers of the brain activate. It can actually calm the brain down. It can also lower heart rate responses during psychosocial stress."

Stress and annoyance appear to be linked. When we're stressed, we seem to be at higher risk for getting annoyed, Rodrigues says. "It does seem that annoyance increases when you're stressed out. You're much more likely to be annoyed if someone cuts you off in traffic when you're running late than when you're in no rush at all. It seems that we have a lower threshold for getting jumpy and irritable when we're stressed out."

If running up against an obstacle when you're trying to achieve a goal puts you at risk for annoyance, stress on top of that practically guarantees it. We're often stressed when the goal we're trying to achieve is pressing or important. This may mean that how annoyed we are is less about the size of the obstacle than about the size of the goal.

Researchers, however, are studying another curious connection. It's likely that the theater shusher had little ability to sympathize with the guy eating the candy. What if the last row of the theater was filled with diabetics who had low blood sugar? Maybe the guy who cut you off in traffic is in an even bigger hurry than you. Empathy would seem to be logically connected to feeling less frustrated in these situations, but it turns out that it may be biologically connected as well.

To test stress reactions, Rodrigues blasted white noise into the ears of 192 UC Berkeley college students. The students got no warning for the first blast. Then, instructions on a TV screen told participants that the next blast would come after a countdown—this gets rid of the surprise but makes people stressed as they wait for the next sound blast. It's called a "classic startle experiment." Stress is measured by how much your heart rate goes up while you wait for the blast.

Rodrigues wanted to know whether there was any significant correlation between a rise in heart rate—how physically stressed a person got waiting for that white noise blast—and a variation in the gene that makes the oxytocin receptor. The participants were also asked to self-report on their stress levels. The hypothesis is that differences in the gene that makes the oxytocin receptor could affect the receptor, which could affect how oxytocin works, which could affect a person's ability to cope with stress.

That's a lot of *coulds*. This is because exactly how this genetic variation affects the oxytocin receptor and how oxytocin responds to that receptor change isn't clear. "We don't know how this particular variation translates to oxytocin," Rodrigues says, "but we're assuming that it is somehow related to oxytocin signaling or sensitivity."

Rodrigues also wanted to know how this oxytocin variation affected a person's ability to empathize. Empathy, as you might imagine, is hard to measure, but one standard approach is a questionnaire. Items on it include "I sometimes try to understand my friends better by imagining how things look from their perspective" and "I really get involved with the feelings of the characters in a novel." Participants were asked to rate each statement according to how much they agreed with it.

Another way to measure empathy is with a multiple-choice test—technically called the Reading the Mind in the Eyes Task (RMET). The college kids were shown about thirty black-and-white photos of strangers' eyes and were asked to select the adjective that "best describes what the individual in the photo is feeling or thinking," according to Rodrigues's study.[2]

Rodrigues found that people with one particular variation in the oxytocin receptor gene scored worse on the empathy test and got more stressed while waiting for the white noise blast. These two characteristics—high stress, low empathy—may be related, Rodrigues says. "There are some old studies that tap into this idea that empathy and stress are on opposite ends of the continuum. It could be something like if we're too consumed by our own distress, we're a bit less capable of recognizing what others are going through." (Previous studies have shown that this genetic variation also makes you more likely to be diagnosed with autism, a syndrome that manifests in displays of anxiousness and social indifference.)

It's jarring—the idea that the difference in a couple of nucleic acid bases on one region of one gene on one chromosome could make you more likely to get stressed and less likely to be able to put yourself in other people's shoes. "I really did come into this research as a huge skeptic," Rodrigues says. "There are so many random gene studies saying there's a dance gene or a divorce gene or that kind of thing. But there's just one oxytocin receptor, and oxytocin is so potent in playing a role in social bonds and stress reactivity. So it would make sense that a variation in the receptor would have an impact on how oxytocin works in our bodies and our brains."

Insofar as oxytocin plays a role in responding to stress, it seems likely that it also is a factor in a person's reactions to irritations. "It's quite possible," says Rodrigues. "Oxytocin can decrease your stress hormone levels. I would definitely put my bet on it that oxytocin would cause less irritability."

A few small studies have looked at how the behavior of people with autism changes after they take an oxytocin nasal spray. One study, published in the *Proceedings of the National Academy of Sciences* in 2010, found that autistic adults seemed to interact more smoothly with others after oxytocin inhalation.[3] It makes you wonder what it would do for candy-averse theater-goers.

Much of what we've learned so far about parts of the brain and fMRIs and so forth would seem to indicate that you become annoyed in your mind. Something unpleasant happens, you get annoyed, and your blood boils. Is that really the right order, though? The oxytocin study suggests a different route—perhaps your blood boils, and then your brain becomes annoyed. Where do feelings start—in the body or the brain? And what are emotions, anyway?

If you're one of those people who finds it hard to express your feelings, you might feel better knowing that humans have a hard time even defining what a feeling is.

"Determining what an emotion is isn't trivial from a scientific perspective," says Randolph Nesse, a psychiatrist and the director of the Evolution and Human Adaptation Program at the University of Michigan. "The attempts to define emotion, in my opinion, have consistently tried to focus on different legs of the elephant: some people say, 'It's physiology,' and other people say, 'No, it's the subject of feeling,' and yet others say, 'No, it's cognition.' There's been a lot of debate about which is primary." Nesse argues that emotions are the whole elephant. They comprise all of those things.

Part of the difficulty in finding a working definition may be that we haven't been working on it that long. Despite the fact that art, music, literature, war, and peace are propelled by emotion, not to mention that emotions are obviously central to our everyday lives, there is not a long tradition of scientifically studying emotion, with a few exceptions. "As the sciences of mind and brain flourished in the twentieth century, interests went elsewhere and the specialties which we loosely group today under neuroscience gave a resolute cold shoulder to emotion research," wrote emotion researcher Antonio Damasio in his book *Descartes' Error*.[4]

The modern inquiry into emotion got a jump-start in the late nineteenth century when science heavyweights Charles

Darwin and William James published their theories on the subject. Darwin tackled emotion in a book called *The Expression of the Emotions in Man and Animals*.[5] He explored emotions through the expressions we make, noting similarities between humans and animals in the external manifestations of our emotional states. He filled the book with pictures of people and animals grimacing, crying, and smiling. There is a particularly unflattering picture of the photographer's wife snarling.

Around the same time, 1884, psychologist-philosopher William James took on the question "What Is an Emotion?" in the journal *Mind*.[6] James wrote that his interest was the human state when a "wave of bodily disturbance of some kind accompanies the perception of the interesting sights or sounds, or the passage of the exciting train of ideas." James was not concerned with things like pleasing arrangements of sounds and colors. His treatise covers only feelings that stir the body, he said, and it seems safe to say that annoyance belongs under his umbrella.

One struggle in defining emotion is finding a way to include the changes that occur in the body, the brain, and the mind (the awareness of the feeling). Here is James's solution: "Our natural way of thinking about these standard emotions is that the mental perception of some fact excites the mental affection called the emotion, and that this latter state of mind gives rise to the bodily expression. My thesis on the contrary is that *the bodily changes follow directly the PERCEPTION of the exciting fact, and that our feeling of the same changes as they occur IS the emotion.*"

Translated: (1) We perceive something; (2) our bodies react—for example, heart rate goes up; we start sweating; we start running; and (3) our minds become aware that we're experiencing an emotion. James sees emotions as the aware- ness of these reflexive bodily changes that occur when we perceive something. Carl Lange was developing a comple- mentary theory around the same time—and what is now called the "James-Lange" theory of emotions was born. More than a hundred years later, scientists still reference this theory in emotion research.[7]

In the last fifteen years, the field of emotion research has been on the upswing. Scientists are not simply studying emo- tion but have again begun to develop theories about what emotion is.

Neuroscientist Joseph LeDoux, in his book *The Emotional Brain*, argues that emotions are different from feelings. "I view emotions as biological functions of the nervous system," he wrote.[8] Emotions are the initial response of the brain to a perception, such as a loud noise or a snake in the road. LeDoux studies how rats process fear by tracing a fear-inducing signal, like a loud noise, from a rat's ear through its brain.

In LeDoux's preferred semantics, a feeling is the part that happens next. Feelings are a secondary reaction that is prompted by this initial brain response, the emotion. Feelings occur when we realize what is going on and start to sweat. While James sees emotions as the perception of changes in our bodies, LeDoux sees *emotions* as what happens initially in the brain and *feelings* as how our minds and bodies react to that initial brain change.

The two-stage process of emotion and feeling that James and LeDoux map out bears on the experience of feeling annoyed. It often seems as if you're annoyed before you're even aware of it. You first feel the bodily signs and symptoms—a flushed face, a rise in blood pressure, sweating, a quickened breathing rate—and then realize, "Oh, yeah, I'm annoyed!" In LeDoux's construct, there would be an initial response in the brain—the emotion—and then that would set off a cascade of effects in the body and the mind, making us aware that we're experiencing the "feeling" of annoyance.

Although scientists may be late to the emotion party, philosophers have been grappling with emotions for millennia, although annoyance is (again) conspicuously absent from the inquiry.

Ronald de Sousa, a philosopher at the University of Toronto, specializes in emotion but hasn't thought much about annoyance. When asked to consider it, his first instinct is that annoyance is what philosophers call a "low-level emotion." Full-fledged emotions, according to de Sousa, have an evaluative dimension. Take anger, for example: "In anger, you have a whole lot of thoughts about perhaps the moral badness or at least the personal badness of something that's been done to you. If I'm angry at you, that means I actually think you did something wrong." By comparison, if we feel annoyed, it's because of something trivial, something that does not violate our moral standards.

Another characteristic of low-level emotion is that it's hard to recreate it in your mind, says de Sousa—it exists only when you are experiencing the changes in your body. Higher-level emotions can be felt more abstractly. For example, you can be angry without feeling your blood pressure go up. Here may be a distinction between irritation and annoyance. Irritation seems to be confined to a sensation in the moment—a merely physiological response, as de Sousa describes. Annoyance, however, may be slightly higher level than de Sousa suggests, in the sense that it does seem possible for us to be annoyed generally with a situation, without feeling the bodily arousal of irritation.

Disgust may be an analogue to annoyance, says de Sousa. Researchers are learning that disgust—once thought to be primitive and low level—is not so simple. A study in *Science* by Hanah Chapman and colleagues looked at people's facial muscles when they reacted to unpleasant things, from pictures of dirty toilets to the taste of a foul liquid to an unfair experience.[9] Dating back to Darwin, facial expressions have been used to characterize emotions. In this case, it turns out that people contort their faces in a similar way when they are in all three situations. A repulsive idea triggers the same muscle response that something physically repulsive does. The idea is that you can be morally disgusted.

When it comes to understanding annoyance, psychiatrist and psychology professor Randolph Nesse frames it this way: "The question I would ask you to consider about annoyance is, can you map it to some particular situation that has recurred over evolutionary time where it would have given an advantage?"

Nesse has written extensively about how emotional responses might be shaped by evolution. "All of these different aspects of emotions—physiology, subjective experience, cognition, behavior, facial expression, the whole bit—they're all coordinated aspects of a response that's useful in certain kinds of situations. This doesn't mean that every emotion has a specific function. Lots of emotions have multiple functions, and there are plenty of overlaps between the functions of different emotions. The bottom line, I argue, is that organisms during the course of evolutionary history have encountered the same kinds of situations with the same kinds of adaptive challenges, over and over again. Those that have a capacity for a somewhat standardized coordinated pattern of responses get a selective advantage."

For irritants—such as chemicals that bother our skin—the adaptive advantage is clear. Too much of an irritant can kill us. Having a mechanism in place to help us avoid them is good for our survival. When the irritant takes on a cognitive nature, however, could the negative feeling that results also be adaptive? "As we pursue a goal, if it's all going well, we feel great," says Nesse. "When we experience an obstacle, we feel frustrated. And I think this may be another emotion that fits pretty nicely into this scheme."

No one in his right mind seeks out situations that will make him feel irritated—it's not a positive feeling—but, according to Nesse, that doesn't mean we'd be better off without annoyance. In fact, Nesse doesn't think any emotions are bad, really: "Everybody assumes that something like annoyance is a bad emotion or we should minimize it because having it is bad. I don't think so, any more than anxiety is bad or sadness is bad or anger is bad—they're all good in terms of their usefulness when they are expressed to the right degree in the right situation."

Nesse suggests all of these negative emotions have some role in helping us survive—they encourage us to avoid things that are bad for us, for example. Maybe annoyance evolved to deter us from engaging in situations that are unpleasant, unpredictable, and out of our control. Or maybe the feeling of annoyance evolved as a by-product of some other, more evolutionarily advantageous traits. The alertness that comes from the dorsal anterior cingulate and the extra energy that comes from stress (and the abatement of oxytocin that lets us focus on selfish needs) all have a clear usefulness for humans. The fact that we accidentally turn on that series of reactions for all sorts of useless things as well may be a side effect.

Perhaps we should be thankful that nature gave us the ability to freak out, no matter what the cause.

"If you think about really simple organisms, they may not have the complex cognitive capacities that we have, but they certainly have things they find aversive, that they want to avoid," says Paul Garrity, a developmental neurobiologist at Brandeis University. It's all part of the drive to survive.

Garrity is interested in what's called chemical nociception, that is, the molecules in cells that recognize irritating chemicals in the environment. These molecules sit in the surfaces of cells, poking out into the extracellular environment. When a noxious chemical floats by, they initiate a cascade of chemical changes inside the cell that protects the cell from damage. Working with fruit flies, Garrity has found evidence that a particular receptor, known as TRPA1, has a long history of helping creatures across the animal kingdom, from sea anemones to fruit flies to humans, detect irritants.

Imagine, for a moment, that you are a fruit fly, and you are hungry. You know what sounds really refreshing? A nice drop of sugar water. Yesterday, there was some near the edge of your enclosure. "Is it still there?" you wonder. You buzz over to that spot, and sure enough, it's there. You lean in for a sip. Yuck. Ptooey. Ick. You recoil in horror. What happened?

Garrity can tell you. He put a little cinnamon in the water. Fruit flies do not like cinnamon. They will refuse to sip sugar water—something they usually seem to enjoy—if it's laced with the spice. They will also turn their proboscises up at wasabi, raw garlic, and mustard. These plants contain chemicals that irritate fruit flies and, not coincidentally, humans as well. In small doses, they are bothersome, rather than harmful. Yet they irritate with a purpose: the feeling is usually a warning that in higher doses, these compounds won't simply annoy you, they will hurt you.

Many chemical irritants—although not all—are irritating because they love electrons. Appropriately named electrophiles, these compounds don't steal electrons; they insist on sharing—which is no less annoying to the compounds they are sharing with. They're like an unwanted houseguest, says Garrity. "They're like the guest who comes and stays and eats your food. They like your house, and they just sort of sit around." That's what electrophiles do.

Electrophiles don't target only the electron-rich. They will try to share electrons with molecules that aren't prone to making donations. "If you take something that is extremely electron-poor, then the donor doesn't have to be as electron-rich as it might otherwise be," says Garrity.

Electrophiles glom onto fats. They put a wrench in the gears of proteins, changing their function, Garrity says, and they latch onto DNA, which can cause mutations. DNA bases are not apt to share their electrons. (This is good news for life on Earth.) "But if you mix them with something that's really starved for electrons, it will find those electrons and form a bond," Garrity says. These chemical irritants that love electrons don't play favorites. "They just go around and muck up whatever."

Yet mucking stuff up isn't what makes these chemicals annoying. They're irritating thanks to a receptor that fruit flies, humans, and, in fact, all invertebrates and vertebrates share. It's called TRPA1 (which stands for "transient receptor potential A1" and is pronounced "trip-a-one"). "In mammals, we think it's primarily a receptor for chemical irritants," says David Julius, a biochemist at the University of California, San Francisco, and the guy who discovered its function.

The job of receptors is to recognize specific chemicals and bind to them. Once a chemical is attached, TRPA1 acts as an alarm, sounding when electrophiles are present in or on our bodies. Without the alarm, this class of chemical irritants wouldn't irritate us. Fruit flies that are genetically modified to lack TRPA1 happily lap up cinnamon sugar water, Garrity showed in a 2010 study in *Nature*.[10] Likewise, Julius showed that pain-sensing nerve fibers from mice lacking the TRPA1 gene do not detect wasabi or other electrophilic irritants.[11] In other words, no TRPA1, no alarm signal. Without TRPA1, life would be less irritating, but it would also be more dangerous.

TRPs are just one type of receptor involved in sending an irritation message. There are different receptors for histamines, which are responsible for irritation from allergies, and acids, such as when lemon juice gets squeezed in your eye. "There's a whole host of receptors that are involved in signaling pain, irritation, and also itch. TRP channels are just one piece of the puzzle," says pain researcher Earl Carstens, from the University of California, Davis. "It's a big puzzle because there are lots of pieces."

TRPs are interesting because they respond to a host of environmental assaults—hot, cold, chemicals. (A cousin of TRPA1—TRPV1—detects the capsaicin in chili peppers.) "It is a truly wide-spectrum irritant receptor," says Carstens of TRPs. Sensitivity to a broad swath of irritants is especially true for TRPA1. David McKemy, who worked in Julius's lab before he got his own at the University of Southern California, says the word *promiscuous* has been thrown around to describe it. "It's more of a question of what doesn't activate it than what does," says McKemy. Horseradish, acrolein (which is found in cigarette smoke and smog), tear gas, and cloves all get a response from TRPA1. Its looseness is unusual for a receptor—most receptors respond only to molecules of a specific shape. Because TRPs generally are sensitive to a wide variety of environmental assaults, they are a hopeful target for pain treatment, says Carstens.

"The way we used to think about pain is that something bad happens and that causes a minor form of skin damage," says Carstens. "And you have these chemicals that are released into the skin that act on pain fibers and cause pain sensation. What this means is that damage has already occurred before you have a chance to respond, and that's how pain used to be thought of. But that's wrong. Pain truly is a warning signal that allows you to do something before any damage occurs."

That makes pain not only useful but essential. Randolph Nesse—who argues for the upsides of negative emotions—also wrote about pain: "Such defenses are analogous to the low oil pressure light on an automobile dashboard. In that case, it is clear the glowing light itself is not the problem; instead the light is a protective response to the problem of low oil pressure." That was from an article titled "What Good Is Feeling Bad?" in a magazine called *Sciences.*[12]

The sensation we feel when a chili pepper is rubbed on our skin or tear gas gets in our eyes isn't due to something being broken; it's the message that something is in danger of being broken. The actual damage—say, DNA getting mutated—doesn't feel like anything.

That's why you need a warning, Garrity says, and TRPA1 is found pretty much everywhere that our bodies meet the outside world: our gut, our nose, our eyes, our skin. When it signals the alarm, the body snaps into operation purge. "One of its main jobs is to help flush stuff out." TRPA1 in our lungs prompts a coughing spell when we inhale pollutants such as cigarette smoke. It makes us cry when we cut onions. Garrity says, "My guess is that it's why you vomit when you eat stuff that's bad for you, and it could be why you get the runs when you have something in your GI tract that isn't necessarily good for you."

This irritant alarm is ancient. Unlike smell and taste, which appear to have evolved multiple times over the course of history, the signal for irritation has been conserved since the Cambrian period. Our ancestors—in fact, the ancestors of all vertebrates and invertebrates—had this protein five hundred million years ago, meaning that these chemicals could have been annoying life on Earth for half a billion years.

Irritation through this receptor may be so constant over the eons because it's difficult to evolve around it. The receptor is turned on by the same mechanism that mucks up the proteins and the lipids in the cells. "You've basically built yourself a sensor that is tremendously good because it recognizes the property that is damaging," says Garrity. The damaging part is the electron sharing. If, in an attempt to go undetected by TRPA1, an electrophile gave up its need for electrons, it would no longer be damaging either.

That the irritant sensor is ubiquitous also makes this class of irritants a good defense mechanism for plants. If everything from insects to humans is annoyed by the same type of compound, it's a pretty foolproof way of warding off a wide range of predators. Plants have taken advantage of this. "Did you ever eat a raw mustard green? At first you chew it, and it tastes like a green. Then after fifteen, twenty seconds, your mouth starts to burn," explains Garrity. That's because mustard greens store two components that, when mixed, form an electrophile. "One compartment has the precursor and the other compartment has an enzyme that breaks down that precursor to create wasabi. When you chew it, you mix together the two ingredients, and you create the reactive electrophiles." This separate packaging is intentional—that way, the electrophiles don't do damage to the plant cells either. The electrophile appears only when the green is attacked—when something is chewing on it.

David Julius demonstrated that electrophiles don't come only from plants. A paper that he and his colleagues published in the *Proceedings of the National Academy of Sciences* showed that electrophiles can also be generated when our tissues are injured—in arthritis, for example.[13] In addition, inflammation can produce electrophiles that activate TRPA1, says Julius.

"That's why you can't necessarily tell whether you just got a reactive electrophile on yourself or whether you maybe did something to yourself," says Garrity. "What you've done is you've basically built something that sees a wide spectrum of the world around you that's damaging, and I'm guessing that's why it's been so conserved." Because tissue damage and wasabi activate the same sensor, these pains feel the same.

The curious thing about physical irritants is that they produce reactions that are nearly indistinguishable from psychological irritants. Get onion juice in your eye, and you start to cry. Your nose runs, and you sniffle. The reaction isn't so different from how most people would respond to an annoying bully hurling insults. "I often wonder why we have the kinds of responses that we have," says Garrity. "The similarities in our responses to chemical irritants and our responses to some kinds of emotional upset are striking—whether they share some mechanistic similarities is unknown at this point, but I wouldn't be surprised if they did. My sense is that what we end up doing is kludging stuff together."

Natural selection is famous for reusing existing systems for new purposes. The jaw bones of reptiles, for example, ultimately became the tiny bones in the middle ear, writes Neil Shubin in his book *Your Inner Fish*.[14]

What if our machinery for responding to chemical irritants is also partly used to respond to cognitive irritants? "That's a bit too speculative for me, I'm afraid," says Julius. "Who knows? I'm not trying to be a reductionist nerd here, but I'm not ready to crawl out on that limb just yet."

Conclusion

According to the International Programs Center of the U.S. Census Bureau, the total population of the world, projected at September 24, 2010, at 19:32 Greenwich Mean Time was 6,870,906,129. That number is significant. It means that on September 24, 2010, there were more than 6.8 billion opinions about what is the most annoying thing in the world.

It's difficult to imagine consensus on this question. Everything is annoying to someone. On the other hand, some things do come close to being universal irritations. Hearing half of a cell phone conversation seems to be one of these super-annoyances.

The main problem with listening to someone else's cell phone call seems to be that it's distracting. Whether we're interested or not, our brains can't help but tune in to the conversation, no matter how banal. If it were merely random noise or an unfamiliar language, we might be able to ignore it—like New Yorkers with an ambulance siren. Tuning out understandable speech is next to impossible, however, because our brains are built to predict what is coming next—especially with speech. With only half of a conversation to work with—a halfalogue, as it is known—there's not enough context. We are constantly frustrated in our effort to anticipate. On top of the cell phone call distracting us from what we'd rather be thinking about, we likely won't even get the satisfaction of making an accurate prediction about the conversation. This may explain why trying to understand why someone on a call would say "He's arriving tomorrow" ten or twelve times in a row is enough to make your head explode. In other words, it's unpleasant—another key component of an annoyance.

Also, even though we know the call will end, the uncertainty of when adds to the annoyance. She must be finished. "He's arriving tomorrow." That's got to be the last one. "He's arriving tomorrow." Please tell me this is the end. "He's arriving tomorrow." Aaargh.

If you're particularly unlucky, you'll be listening to someone whose voice captures some of the same sound qualities as fingernails on a chalkboard. That sound is supremely annoying, perhaps because it has similar qualities to a human scream.

On top of everything else, maybe you're working with a cognitive overlay or two. Your ex, let's say, logged many hours halfalogueing in your presence, and you always fought about it, but now you miss her, and you wonder whether she misses you, and so forth, and so on.

The inevitable question is, does the knowledge of what makes a super-annoyance annoying provide any hints on how to overcome it? Maybe.

We know that socially unacceptable things are annoying. Trimming your nails in public seems to fall into that category for a lot of people. So does talking on a cell phone in a crowded public space. You could try to convince yourself that because cell phones are so ubiquitous and so essential to modern life, it's unfair to think of them as no longer socially acceptable. You could try that.

We know that things that keep us from accomplishing a task are annoying. If the call distracts you from giving your full attention to your workout or completing that difficult crossword puzzle, you could try to convince yourself that the task at hand isn't all that important, and a temporary distraction won't matter that much. You could try that.

If the woman on the treadmill next to you in the gym is having an interminable call with her boyfriend, you could try focusing on something else. "There is only me and the stationary bike. I am one with the stationary bike. I hear nothing but the whirring of the gears. I sense nothing but the pumping of my blood." That might work.

You could take the Zinedine Zidane approach and head-butt the person on the cell phone—that might make you feel better, until you get arrested. Maybe just thinking about doing it will help ease your irritation.

Or you could adopt the attitude of the Ifaluk islanders and simply accept the annoyance, realize that it's an inherent component of the social milieu in which you find yourself, and move on. You could try that.

You could try all of those things, but based on our extensive research, none of these strategies works that well. They might make you feel better momentarily, but the things that bug us do so in a way that transcends reason. You know that your reaction to this minor unpleasantness is out of proportion, yet you can't help but get annoyed. And once you're annoyed about being annoyed, it's all over. This is terminal annoyance.

So, as a last-ditch effort, remember that bad feelings—on the whole—usually aren't so bad. They signal that something is wrong, which throws into relief that things usually aren't. If overhearing an annoying halfalogue is your biggest problem, buy some earplugs and be thankful.

Acknowledgments

L ong acknowledgments are annoying. Brace yourself.

We are grateful for the many people who took the time to talk with us during this project. You can see their names scattered throughout this book. We would particularly like to thank Robert Hogan and Paul Connolly for their help with developing a scientifically credibly annoyingness test; Linda Bartoshuk for her interest in scaling annoyingness; Carol Tavris for her helpful suggestions; Chris Joyce, Sarah Brookhart, Janet Zipser, Corey Dean, Erik Tarloff, Sandy Blakeslee, Alta Charo, and Michael Lemonick for contributing stories about what annoyed them; and Sarah Varney for her wonderful research on cultural annoyances.

F. L. is grateful for the mentorship and generous support of Ira Flatow, her boss at *Science Friday*, and the intelligent guidance of Annette Heist, the show's senior producer. J. P. thanks his NPR editors Alison Richards and Anne Gudenkauf for their support. He also would like to thank NPR president Vivian Schiller for her enthusiasm about this project.

We also gratefully acknowledge the encouragement and support of our agent, Jim Levine, and his colleagues and staff at Levine Greenberg.

This book would never have happened without Eric Nelson, our editor at Wiley. A few years ago, he e-mailed J. P. out of the blue asking if he'd like to write a book. "No," J. P. replied without a moment's hesitation. Eric evidently had a better crystal ball on his desk than J. P. did.

That brings us to a paragraph that's hard to write in the third person, so Joe will take it from here. This book was Flora's idea. People who know me have trouble believing that, because for some reason, most of my coworkers, friends, and certainly my immediate family believe that I have more practical knowledge about how to be annoying than anyone they've ever met. But Flora has had many interesting, provocative, clever ideas in the time that I've known her, and this book was one of them. She was kind enough to let me write it with her.

Many friends deserve thanks for their interest and positive feedback: Doris Palca, Soji Adeyi, Gaby Newes-Adeyi, Claire Wyman, Roland Kanaar, Bob O'Rourke, and Kim Darnell.

I was lucky enough to have two splendid fellowships while this book was being planned and written. I was science writer in residence for six months at the Huntington Library and

Botanical Garden, where I was able to pester the staff with annoying questions. Special thanks to Huntington president Steve Koblik (who I think has finally forgiven me for failing to catch an egregious spelling error when I "proof read" one of his books), Dan Lewis, Roy Ritchie, Susan Turner-Lowe, and most especially Laurie Sowd.

The other fellowship was as a visiting media scholar at the Hoover Institution, where I spent an extremely productive week on probably the most unusual project ever pursued at that institution. Thanks to Henry Miller, Mandy MacCalla, and David Brady.

I would like to thank my children, Sam and Jacob, for putting up with their annoying father, and my wife, Kathy Hudson, who had an unconventional but nonetheless effective way of helping me write this book. I'm extremely grateful for her love.

Notes

Introduction: Cell Phones

1. L. L. Emberson, G. Lupyan, M. H. Goldstein, and M. J. Spivey, "Overheard Cell-Phone Conversations: When Less Speech Is More Distracting," *Psychological Science* 21(10) (2010): 1383–1388.
2. Ibid.
3. A. Monk, J. Carrol, P. Parker, and M. Blythe, "Why Are Mobile Phones Annoying?" *Behaviour and Information Technology* 23 (2004): 33–41.
4. Mark Twain, "A Telephonic Conversation," *Atlantic Magazine* (June 1880) via Mark Liberman, "That Queerest of All the Queer Things," Language Log (January 18, 2010), http://itre.cis.upenn.edu/~myl/languagelog/archives/000641.html.
5. Mark Liberman, "Mind-Reading Fatigue," Language Log (November 8, 2003), http://itre.cis.upenn.edu/~myl/languagelog/archives/000095.html.
6. Emberson, Lupyan, Goldstein, and Spivey, "Overheard Cell-Phone Conversations."

2. A Case of Mistaken Intensity

1. Christopher Columbus, *The Journal: Account of the First Voyage and Discovery of the Indies,* trans. Marc A. Beckwith and Luciano F. Farina (Rome: Libreria dello Stato, 1992).

2. R. H. Cichewicz and P. A. Thorpe, "The Antimicrobial Properties of Chile Peppers (Capsicum Species) and Their Uses in Mayan Medicine," *Journal of Ethnopharmacolgy* 52(2) (June 1996): 61–70.

3. N. L. Jones, S. Shabib, and P. M. Sherman, "Capsaicin as an Inhibitor of the Growth of the Gastric Pathogen Helicobacter Pylori," *FEMS Microbiology Letters* 146(2) (January 15, 1997): 223–227.

4. P. Rozin and D. Schiller, "The Nature and Acquisition of a Preference for Chili Pepper in Humans," *Motivation and Emotion* 4(1) (1980): 77–101.

5. "McDonald's USA Nutrition Facts for Popular Menu Items," www.scribd.com/doc/222559/McDonalds-Nutrition-Facts.

3. Fingernails on a Chalkboard

1. Lynn Halpern, Randolph Blake, and James Hillenbrand, "Psychoacoustics of a Chilling Sound," *Perception and Psychophysics* (1986): 77–80.

2. Dogs can hear pitches up to 40,000 Hz; chinchillas have a hearing range like ours; mice ears register sound up to 91,000 Hz (but they have trouble with frequencies under 1,000 Hz); catfish are limited to frequencies under 4,000 Hz.

3. B. Kruger, "An Update on the External Ear Resonance in Infants and Young Children," *Ear and Hearing* 8(6) (1987): 333–336.

4. Mark Leibovich, "Obama's Partisan, Profane Confidant Reins It In," *New York Times*, January 25, 2009, p. 1.

5. Kruger, "An Update on the External Ear Resonance."

6. J. Vos and G. F. Smoorenburg, "Penalty for Impulse Noise, Derived from Annoyance Ratings for Impulse and Road-Traffic Sounds," *Journal of the Acoustical Society of America* 77(1) (1985): 193–201; T. Hashimoto and S. Hatano, "Roughness Level as a Measure for Estimating Unpleasantness: Modification of Roughness Level by Modulation Frequencies," *Proceedings of the Inter-Noise 94 Conference*, Yokohama, Japan (1994): 887–892.

4. Skunked

1. William Wood, "The History of Skunk Defensive Secretion Research," *Chemical Educator* 4 (1999): 44–50.
2. Eric Block, *Garlic and Other Alliums: The Lore and the Science* (Cambridge, UK: Royal Society of Chemistry), 2009.
3. Rachel Herz, *The Scent of Desire: Discovering Our Enigmatic Sense of Smell* (New York: HarperCollins), 2007.
4. Rachel S. Herz and Julia von Clef, "The Influence of Verbal Labeling on the Perception of Odors: Evidence for Olfactory Illusions?" *Perception* 30(3) (2001): 381–391.
5. Paul Krebaum, "Lab Method Deodorizes a Skunk-Afflicted Pet," *Chemical & Engineering News* 71(42) (1993): 90.
6. The recipe and directions can be found at http://home.earthlink.net/~skunkremedy/home/.

5. Bugged by Bugs: An Epic Bugging

1. Daniel J. Simons and Christopher F. Chabris, "Gorillas in Our Midst: Sustained Inattentional Blindness for Dynamic Events," *Perception* 28 (1999): 1059–1074.
2. Entomological Society of America, "Frequently Asked Questions on Entomology," http://www.entsoc.org/resources/faq#triv4.
3. Charles Darwin, *On the Origin of Species* (London: John Murray), 1859.
4. Francesco Facchinetti, "Sarà un campionato super, parola nostra," *Sorrisi e Canzoni*, August 24, 2007, http://archivio.sorrisi.com/sorrisi/personaggi/art023001038259.jsp.
5. Diego Torres, "El fútbol empieza en la calle," *El Pais*, March 1, 2010, http://www.elpais.com/articulo/deportes/futbol/empieza/calle/elpepidep/20100301elpepidep_18/Tes.

6. Who Moved Their Cheese?

1. "A Possible Mendelian Explanation for a Type of Inheritance Apparently Non-Mendelian in Nature," *Science* 40 (December 18, 1914): 904–906.

8. Dissonant

1. Pantelis Vassilakis, "Perspectives in Systematic Musicology: Auditory Roughness as a Means of Musical Expression," *Selected Reports in Ethnomusicology* 12 (2005): 119–144.
2. J. P. Van de Geer, W. J. M. Levelt, and R. Plomp, "The Connotation of Musical Consonance," *Acta Psychologica* 20 (1962): 308–319.
3. Thomas Fritz, Sebastian Jentschke, Nathalie Gosselin, et al., "Universal Recognition of Three Basic Emotions in Music." *Current Biology* 19(7) (2009): 573–576.

9. Breaking the Rules

1. Sarah F. Brosnan and Frans B. M. de Waal, "Monkeys Reject Unequal Pay," *Nature* 425 (September 18, 2003): 297–299.
2. O. L. Tinklepaugh, "An Experimental Study of Representative Factors in Monkeys," *Journal of Comparative Psychology* 8(3) (1928): 197–236.
3. Sarah Brookhart, personal communication with the author.

10. He's Just Not That Annoyed by You

1. D. Felmlee, "From Appealing to Appalling: Disenchantment with a Romantic Partner," *Sociological Perspectives* 44(3) (2001): 263–280.
2. R. S. Miller, "We Always Hurt the Ones We Love: Aversive Interactions in Close Relationships," in R. M. Kowalski, ed., *Aversive Interpersonal Behaviors* (New York: Plenum Press, 1997), 11–29, esp. p. 19.

11. Better Late Than Never Doesn't Apply Here

1. Catherine Lutz, *Unnatural Emotions: Everyday Sentiments on a Micronesian Atoll and Their Challenge to Western Theory* (Chicago: University of Chicago Press, 1988), 82.
2. Reuters Life! "Quiet Please! Noise Irks Japan's Commuters the Most," January 15, 2010, http://in.reuters.com/article/idINIndia -45415320100115.

3. Michael Ross and Qi Wang, "Why We Remember and What We Remember: Culture and Autobiographical Memory," *Perspectives on Psychological Science* 5 (2010): 401.

4. Robert V. Levine, *A Geography of Time: On Tempo, Culture, and the Pace of Life* (New York: Basic Books, 1997), 5.

5. Ibid., 6.

6. Edward T. Hall, *The Hidden Dimension* (New York: Anchor Books, 1966).

12. When Your Mind Becomes a Foreign Country

1. Camille L. Julien, Jennifer C. Thompson, Sue Wild, et al., "Psychiatric Disorders in Preclinical Huntington's Disease," *Journal of Neurology, Neurosurgery, and Psychiatry* 78 (2007): 939–943.

2. J. S. Snowden, Z. C. Gibbons, A. Blackshaw, et al., "Social Cognition in Frontotemporal Dementia and Huntington's Disease," *Neuropsychologia* 41(6) (2003): 688–701.

3. J. S. Snowden, N. A. Austin, S. Sembi, J. C. Thompson, D. Craufurd, and D. Neary "Emotion Recognition in Huntington's Disease and Frontotemporal Dementia." *Neuropsychologia* 46(11) (September 2008): 2638–2649.

4. S. Klöppel, C. M. Stonnington, P. Petrovic, et al., "Irritability in Pre-Clinical Huntington's Disease." *Neuropsychologia* 48(2) (January 2010): 549–557.

13. The Annoyed Brain

1. Dana and David Dornslife, Cognitive Neuroscience Imaging Center, http://brainimaging.usc.edu/index.php?topic=forsubjects.

2. R. A. Cohen, R. Paul, T. M. Zawacki, D. J. Moser, L. Sweet, and H. Wilkinson, "Emotional and Personality Changes following Cingulotomy," *Emotion* 1 (2001): 38–50.

14. False Alarms

1. Larry J. Young, "Being Human: Love: Neuroscience Reveals All," *Nature* 457(148) (January 8, 2009): 148.

2. Sarina M. Rodrigues, Laura R. Saslow, Natalia Garcia, Oliver P. John, and Dacher Keltner, "Oxytocin Receptor Genetic Variation Relates to Empathy and Stress Reactivity in Humans," *Proceedings of the National Academy of Science*, November 23, 2009, www.pnas.org/content/early/2009/11/18/0909579106.full .pdf+html.

3. Elissar Andaria, Jean-René Duhamela, Tiziana Zallab, Evelyn Herbrechtb, Marion Leboyerb, and Angela Sirigua, "Promoting Social Behavior with Oxytocin in High-Functioning Autism Spectrum Disorders," *Proceedings of the National Academy of Sciences* 107(9) (March 2, 2010): 4389–4394.

4. Antonio Damasio, *Descartes' Error: Emotion, Reason, and the Human Brain* (New York: Grosset/Putnam, 1994).

5. Charles Darwin, *The Expression of the Emotions in Man and Animals* (Great Britain: John Murray, 1872).

6. William James, "What Is an Emotion?" *Mind* 9 (1884): 188–205.

7. For a detailed time line of emotion research, see Tim Dalgleish, "The Emotional Brain," *Nature Reviews Neuroscience* 5 (July 2004): 583–589.

8. Joseph LeDoux, *The Emotional Brain: The Mysterious Underpinnings of Emotional Life* (New York: Touchstone, 1996).

9. Chapman, H. A., D. A. Kim, J.M. Susskind, and A. K. Anderson, "In Bad Taste: Evidence for the Oral Oorigins of Moral Disgust," *Science* 323 (2009):1222–1226.

10. K. Kang, S. R. Pulver, V. C. Panzano, et al., "Analysis of Drosophila TRPA1 Reveals an Ancient Origin for Human Chemical Nociception," *Nature* 464 (2010): 597–600.

11. D. Bautista, S. Jordt, T. Nikai, et al., "TRPA1 Mediates the Inflammatory Action of Environmental Irritants and Proalgesic Agentsm," *Cell* 124 (2006): 1269–1282.

12. Randolph Nesse, "When Good Is Feeling Bad: The Evolutionary Benefits of Psychic Pain," *Sciences* (November/December 1991): 30–37.

13. M. Trevisani, J. Siemens, S. Materazzi et al., "4-Hydroxynonenal, an Endogenous Aldehyde, Causes Pain and Neurogenic Inflammation through Activation of the Irritant Receptor TRPA1," *Proceedings of the National Academy of Sciences* 104 (2007): 13519–135124.

14. Neil Shubin, *Your Inner Fish: A Journey into the 3.5-Billion-Year History of the Human Body* (New York: Vintage Books, 2009).

Index